Knitting for Fun

ERRATA

On page 61 the pattern under the heading 'Yellow Sweater' is illustrated on the same page. The publishers regret that the photograph shown is a blue sweater instead of a yellow one, but wish to reassure readers that the photograph does illustrate the pattern in all respects except color.

Knitting
for
Fun

By
Diana Biggs

Octopus Books

Frontispiece : Poncho (see page 41)

Photographs by Jason Biggs

First published in 1973 by Octopus Books Limited
59 Grosvenor Street, London W I

© 1973 Octopus Books Limited

ISBN 0 7064 0270 7

Produced by Mandarin Publishers Limited
14 Westlands Road, Quarry Bay, Hong Kong
and printed in Hong Kong

Contents

Introduction

Both Knitting and Fun can mean different things to different people. In this book, I have tried to cover all the meanings of both.

To some, knitting is a soothing and enjoyable thing to do, to others it is an art form and a craft. For many it is an economical way to have things one could not afford to buy, yet which are fun to have. Seeing an intricate pattern, growing stitch by stitch, will give great pleasure to the expert and enthusiastic knitter. An effective and striking possession will please those who require almost instant results, if it can be made in the shortest time possible.

Most of us find fun in giving, more so when the gift is received with pleasure. While many love clothes which are fun to wear, a child will get endless enjoyment from a favourite toy. When something you have made for your own home is admired by friends, that can be a rather nice feeling. Last, but certainly not least, many people help to provide for fetes and bazaars in aid of charity. There are many things to make which will find favour with those who visit the fete and give pleasure to the organisers by swelling the funds.

While some things in this book will require a little patience, there are many more easily within the powers of the beginner. Quite a number are based on a rectangle, with no shaping at all, but none that could be called 'square'.

It is my hope that the reader will find everything interesting and useful and a pleasure to make.

Comparative knitting needle sizes

English	000	00	0	1	2		3	4	5	6	7	8	9	10	11	12	13	14
American		15	13	12	11	10 1/2	10	9	8	7	6	5	4	3	2	1	0	00

Knitting needle sizes are not yet uniform in all countries and it is not always easy to decide which size is required. This chart tells you how English and American sizes compare. The important thing in all patterns will be the tension at which the item should be knitted. It is essential to obtain the correct tension in order to make the size given. Change needles to obtain the correct tension, as knitters vary, some people knitting loosely and some tightly. In all patterns in this book, the English needle size is given first, followed by the equivalent American needle size, given in brackets.

Comparative wool chart

All items in this book have been made up in specific yarns. The best results will always be obtained if the stated yarn is used.

When a particular yarn is not obtainable in any country, the following chart may be used as a guide to a second choice.

If it is essential to use a different yarn, it is most important to make a tension check, using a suitable needle size for the yarn involved. Yarns of the same thickness can vary in the number of yards there are in a ball, so the quantity of yarn required may vary if the yarn has to be changed.

United Kingdom	Australia	Canada	S. Africa	U.S.A.
EMU	All yarns mentioned are on sale in all above countries and in each case are sold under the EMU brand name.			
LISTER	Yarns should be readily available in all countries. In case of difficulty use:			
Lavenda Double Crepe	Standard D.K. in all cases			
Lavenda D.K.	Standard D.K. in all cases			
Prema Bulky Knitting	Standard Double Double Knitting in all cases			
Lavenda 4-ply	Standard 4-ply in all cases			
Aran Knitting Wool	Standard Triple Knitting in all cases			
Lavenda Double Six	Standard Triple Knitting in all cases			
LEE TARGET MOTORAVIA D.K.	Standard D.K. in all cases			

United Kingdom	Australia	Canada	S. Africa	U.S.A.
EMU MACHINE WASHABLE D.K.	Often available in all countries, in case of difficulty use Standard D.K. in all cases			
MAHONY	Should be readily available in all countries In U.S.A. Sold under the Bernat Label			
Blarney Bainin				Bernat Blarney Spun
Blarney Berella				Bernat Blarney Beralla
PATONS				
Trident D.K.	Standard D.K. in all cases			
Patons D.K.	Standard D.K. in all cases			
Limelight Double Crepe	Standard D.K. in all cases			
SIRDAR				
Candytwist	Standard Triple Knitting in all cases			
Pullman	Standard Double Double Knitting in all cases			
Sirdar D.K.	Standard D.K. in all cases			
Topline Nylon D.K.	Standard D.K. Nylon in all cases			
Talisman 4-ply	Standard 4-ply in all cases			
TWILLEY	All yarns should be available in all countries			
WENDY				
4-ply Nylonised	Standard 4-ply in all cases			
Wendy D.K.	Standard D.K. in all cases			
Tricel Nylon D.K.	Standard Tricel Nylon D.K. in all cases			
D.K. Nylonised	Standard D.K. in all cases			
Diabolo D.K.	Standard D.K. in all cases			

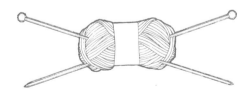

Abbreviations used in this book

Abbreviations are used in knitting patterns to make instructions easier and less tedious to follow. Many of them are easily recognisable to most knitters. Make sure you do understand them all before you begin to knit. This will save you time and trouble once you have started.

K.,	Knit
p.,	purl
g.st.	garter stitch.
st.st.	stocking stitch.
st(s).	stitch(es).
inc.,	increase.
dec.,	decrease.
alt.,	alternate.
foll.,	following.
beg.,	beginning.
cont.,	continue.
patt.,	pattern.
tog.,	together.
p.u.k.,	Pick up loop lying before and k. into back of it.
next st.,	
rep.,	repeat.
rem.,	remaining.
p.s.s.o.,	pass slipped st. over.
sl.,	slip.
t.b.l.,	through back of loop(s).
d.m.st.,	double moss stitch.
m.st.,	moss stitch.
c.n.,	cable needle.
sl.1, k.1, p.s.s.o.,	slip 1, knit 1, pass slipped stitch over.
K.b.1 or P.b.1.,	knit or purl into back of next st.
T2F.,	(Twist 2 Front) K. into front of 2nd st. on left hand needle, then k. first st. and sl. both from needle tog.
T2B.,	(Twist 2 Back) K. into back of 2nd st. on left hand needle, then into front of first st. and sl. both off tog.
Cable 5.,	Sl. next 2 sts. on to c.n. and leave at front, sl. next st. on to 2nd c.n., and leave at back, k. next 2 sts., then p.1 from back c.n., and k.2 from front c.n.
C3R.,	(Cross 3 right) Sl. next st. on to c.n. and leave at back, k.2, then p.1 from c.n.
C3L.,	(Cross 3 Left) Sl. next 2 sts. on to c.n. and leave at front, p.1, then k.2 from c.n.
DC9.,	(Double cable 9) Sl. next 3 sts. on to c.n. and leave at back, k.1, then k.3 from c.n., k.1, sl. next st. on to c.n., and leave at front, k.3, then k.1 from c.n.

K.1B.	Knit next st. but insert needle into st. in row below, allowing st. above to drop from needle.
y.fwd.	yarn forward.
y.r.n.	yarn round needle.
y.o.n.	yarn over needle.
w.fwd.	wool forward.
w.o.n.	wool over needle.
w.r.n.	wool round needle.
w.b.	wool back.
K.f.b. or p.f.b.,	K. or P. into front and back of next st.
3-in-1.,	K.1, p.1, k.1 all into next st.
C6B or C6F.,	(Cable 5 Back or cable 6 Front) Sl. next 3 sts. on to c.n., and leave at back, or front, k.3, then k.3 from c.n.
TR.,	(Twist Right) Sl. next 2 sts. on to c.n. leave at back, k.1, then k.2 from c.n.
T.L.,	(Twist Left) Sl. next st. on to c.n., leave at front, k.2, then k.1 from c.n. These twists are used in the Lobster claw and honeycomb patterns.
C2B.,	(Cable 2 back) Sl. next st. on to c.n., and leave at back, k.b.1., p.1 from c.n.
C2F.,	(Cable 2 front) Sl. next st. on to c.n., and leave at front, p.1, then k.b.1 from c.n.
C4B.,	(Cable 4 back) Sl. next 2 sts. on to c.n., leave at back, k.2, then k.2 from c.n.
C4F.,	(Cable 4 front) As C4B but leave 2 sts. on c.n. at front.
CP7.,	(Claw Patt. 7) Sl. next 2 sts. on to c.n., leave at back, k.1, then k.2 from c.n., k. next st., then sl. foll. st. on to c.n., leave at front, k.2, then k.1 from c.n.
Cross 5.,	S. next 3 sts. on to c.n., leave at back, k.2, now pass the p. st. from other end of c.n. back on to left hand needle, bring c.n. to front, p.1 from left hand needle and lastly, k.2 from c.n.
M.B.,	(Make Bobble) Into next st., work k.1, (w.fwd., k.1) twice, turn and p. these 5 sts., turn, k.5, turn p.5, turn. Now sl. 2nd, 3rd and 4th sts. over 1st and off needle, then k. tog. the rem. 2 sts. t.b.l. On next row, k. the st. over bobble tightly.
R.S.,	(Rich Stitch) As given in pattern concerned.
C6R.,	(Cable 6 right) Sl. next 4 sts. on to c.n., leave at back, k.2, sl.2 p. sts. from c.n. to left hand needle, bring c.n. to front, p.2 from left hand needle, then k.2 from c.n.
C6L.,	(Cable 6 left) Sl. next 2 sts. on to c.n., leave at front, sl. next 2 sts. on to 2nd c.n., leave at back, k.2 from left hand needle, p.2 from back c.n., k.2 from front c.n.
M.L.,	(Make Loop) Insert point of right hand needle into next st. and wind yarn over point of needle and first finger of left hand twice, then over needle again, draw through three loops. Place these 3 loops back on left hand needle and k. tog. t.b.l.
ins.,	Inches.

Trims and Finishes

Even though you make something from a pattern which many other people may be using, your own individual touch can be given, to make it quite different.

Your own choice of colour is only the beginning. After that, the plainest knitting can be trimmed very easily. Fringes, cords, tassels and pompons are simple to make. If Fair Isle knitting is difficult for you to do, patterns can be added to stocking stitch knitting by using Swiss darning. It is not a method to use for a very complicated, all-over pattern, but for borders and motifs it is ideal.

TO MAKE TASSELS

Take a piece of cardboard which is the length you wish to make the finished tassel. Wind yarn round until you have the required thickness. With a large eyed needle and matching yarn, secure the yarn to the loops at one end. Bind through the loops, fasten off and leave the end of yarn. This can join the tassel to the item to be trimmed.

With a length of matching yarn, bind round all threads about a quarter of the length from the top. Thread the yarn through needle and draw down to the lower end. Cut loops at lower end and trim evenly.

TO MAKE POMPONS

Cut two circles of firm cardboard. The diameter should be that required for the finished pompon. Cut a circle out of each piece of cardboard at centre and place the pieces together. Wind yarn through the centre hole and round both pieces of cardboard until the centre hole is completely filled.

Thread a large eyed needle with matching yarn. Cut the loops between the two circles of cardboard and separate a little. Bind yarn tightly between the circles in the centre and tie firmly. Remove cardboard and trim pompon evenly.

TO MAKE TWISTED CORDS

Take several lengths of yarn. They should be three times the length required for the finished cord and about half as thick. Secure one end firmly and taking the other end, twist until it forms a firm, tight cord. Fold in half and allow the two halves to twist together from the centre. Tie a knot at each end and trim to make a tassel. For a two colour cord, the same method is used but it is best to use half the length in one colour and the second half in another. Tie in a knot at the centre. When the twisted strands run together, the colours will appear alternately in stripes.

TO MAKE FRINGES

The thickness of a fringe will depend on the number of strands used.

Cut strands of yarn a little more than twice the length of the required fringe. Take two or more strands, according to the thickness wanted in the finished fringe. Fold the strands in half and with a crochet hook, draw the fold through the edge to be trimmed. Then draw the ends through the fold and pull tight.

If a tasseled fringe is required, knot each piece a quarter of the length down from the top. Make sure the knots make a level line.

TO DO SWISS DARNING

Any cross stitch chart or one used for tapestry can be followed. You can work your own motifs and borders out on squared paper. If you do this, remember that the stitch will be a little wider than it is long, so the final result will be contracted in length. This will not effect the appearance of a balanced Fair Isle design but if you are using a flower or figure motif, they can appear rather squat and look less attractive.

When planning charts for figures, animals and flowers, I find it best to elongate the design a little, although it is easily enough regulated while working. The stitches are simple to put in and take out.

Swiss darning looks as if it has been knitted in but is added to stocking stitch afterwards and follows the path of the knitted stitch.

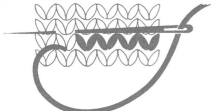

Thread a large eyed, blunt pointed needle with the required yarn in the same thickness as the original work. Insert the needle into the base of the stitch to be covered, from the back of the work. Pass the needle behind the two threads forming the stitch and down again into the base of the stitch from the front of the work. Continue in this way until the stitches for the pattern have been covered in the correct colours.

The Fair Isle mitts and the embroidered patches in the Hexagon patchwork bedspread were worked in this way. Charts are given for both on the appropriate pages.

TO DO GRAFTING

This is a method which can be used to join two sets of stitches. The finished result looks like a row of knitting and there is no ridge.

The toes of socks and stockings are usually finished in this way and the shoulders of sweaters can be grafted. The two sets of stitches should be equal in number.

Place the two sets of stitches on their own needles together with right sides outside. The points of the needles should be to the right hand side and the end of wool at the back needle at the right.

Thread yarn into a large eyed needle. Insert the needle purlwise through the loop of the first stitch on the front needle but do not slip the stitch off the needle. Insert the needle knitwise through the first stitch on the back needle, but do not slip off.

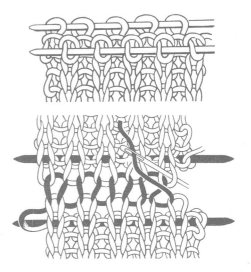

* Insert needle knitwise through first stitch on front needle and slip off needle, then purlwise through the second stitch on front needle, but do not slip off. Now insert wool needle purlwise through first stitch on back needle and slip off, then through second stitch on back needle, knitwise and do not slip off. Repeat from * until all stitches are worked off both knitting needles. Fasten off.

Headlines, footnotes and handouts

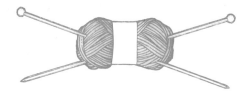

Hats and caps for fun and fashion,
gaily striped stockings for the young, but made in one
colour, all good and warm for country walkers
in winter.

Tiny slippers for a baby and a toddler and gloves and
mitts for summer and winter. These are the
small things to add a touch of colour
or warmth to life and yet so easy to make

Toddlers' slippers

for colour illustration, see page 15

Children's feet seem to grow so quickly, it is hard to keep up with them. Make the next size of slippers from just a little thick wool and keep those toddling feet warm

Materials: Two 50 gramme balls of Sirdar Pullman in White and 1 in Turquoise;
a pair of No. 7(6) knitting needles.

Tension: 5 sts. to 1 inch.

Measurements: Back of heel to toe: 5 ins.

Abbreviations: See page 10

TO MAKE
With Turquoise, cast on 39 sts. and knit 1 row. Now work in patt.
1st row: K.1, s.k.p.o., * k.9, sl.2, k.1, p.s.s.o., rep. from * ending k.9, k.2 tog., k.1.
2nd row: K.1, * p.1, k.4, (k.1, w.r.n., k.1) all into next st., k.4, rep. from * to last 2 sts., p.1, k.1. Change to White.
3rd and 4th rows: As 1st and 2nd rows. Repeat these 4 rows once again then repeat rows 1 and 2. Change to white and knit 1 row. Work 5 rows k.1, p.1, rib. K. 1 row. Begin shaping.
1st row: K.19, p.u.k., k.1, p.u.k., k.19.
2nd and alt. rows: Knit.
3rd row: K.19, p.u.k., k.3, p.u.k., k.19.
5th row: K.19, p.u.k., k.5, p.u.k., k.19.
Continue to work in this way until 11 sts. are worked at centre for toe. Now work 10 rows in garter stitch. Dec. 1 st. at each end of next 2 rows. Cast off. Press. Join back and foot seam. Make another slipper to match.

Baby slippers

for colour illustration, see page 15

However tiny you are you can always do with some slippers. This pair will be the neatest and sweetest you have made

Materials: 1 oz. Lister Lavenda Double Crepe;
a pair of No. 11(2) and a set of 4 No. 10(3) double pointed knitting needles.

Tension: 6½ sts. and 9 rows to 1 inch on No. 10(3) needles.

Measurements: Length of foot: 4 ins. To fit 2nd size.

Abbreviations: See Page 10

TO MAKE

With No. 11(2) needles, cast on 11 sts. for instep. Beg. with a k. row, work 4 rows st.st. Change to two No. 10(3) needles and work a further 4 rows. Make a hem.
9th row: Fold work in half. With p. side inside, k. tog., 1 st. from needle and one from cast on edge to end of row. Beg. with a p. row, work 12 more rows st.st. Dec. 1 st. at each end of next row. K. 1 row, then dec. 1 st. at each end of next row. Break wool and leave these sts. on needle. With 3rd No. 10(3) needle, cast on 13 sts. then, with right side of work facing, pick up and knit 15 sts. along right-hand side of instep. With free needle, knit the 7 sts. from instep, then with 3rd needle, pick up and knit 15 sts. along other side of strip. Turn and cast on 13 sts. Work in rows, using 4 needles. Beg. with a k. row and work 5 rows reversed st.st. **Next row:** (Right side) K. tog. 1 st. from needle and 1 from cast on edge along 13 sts. Now k. tog. 1 st. from needle and one from back of pick-up sts. then continue to make hem round top of slipper to end of row. Beg. with a p. row, work 8 rows in st.st., working all sts. on to one needle on last row.
Foot shaping: Change to reversed st.st.
1st and alt. rows: S.k.p.o., k. to last 2 sts., k.2 tog.
2nd row: P.21, (p.2 tog., p.4) 3 times, p.2 tog., p.20. **4th row:** P.19, (p.2 tog., p.3) 3 times, p.2 tog., p.19.
6th row: P.17, (p.2 tog., p.2) 3 times, p.2 tog., p.18. **8th row:** P.15, (p.2 tog., p.1) 3 times, p.2 tog., p.17. Cast off.

TO MAKE UP

Fold cast off edge in half and join with flat seam. Join back seam. Press seams.

Big tammy

A big tammy is tops for fashion just now, but if you prefer the normal beret, then the instructions cater for that too

Materials: 3 ozs. Sirdar Double Knitting wool in Blue and 1 oz. each of Red and Brown; a pair each of Nos. 11(2) and 9(4) knitting needles.

Tension: 6 sts. and 8 rows to 1 inch on No. 9(4) needles.

Measurements: To fit an average head.

Abbreviations: See Page 10

TO MAKE
With No. 11(2) needles and Blue, cast on 106 sts. and work in k.1, p.1 rib for 1½ ins. Change to Brown and k. 2 rows. Change to Blue. **1st inc. row:** * K.6, p.u.k., rep. from * to last 4 sts., k.4. Purl 1 row.
Pattern Row: (right side) * W.r.n., sl.1, k.1, p.s.s.o., rep. from * to last st., k.1. Purl 1 row. Change to Red and knit 2 rows. Change to Blue and knit 1 row.
2nd inc. row: * P.5, p.u.k., rep. from * to last 3 sts., p.3. Now rep. patt. row, then purl 1 row. Change to Brown and knit 2 rows. Change to Blue and knit 1 row.
3rd inc. row: * P.6, p.u.k., rep. from * to last 3 sts., p.3. Rep. patt. row. Purl 1 row, change to red and knit 2 rows, change to Blue and knit 1 row. Cont. to keep striped patt. correct and work until 3 more increase rows have been worked.
Note: For yellow beret, work 1 more decrease row only. Now decrease. Begin decreasing for yellow beret on 3rd dec. row.
1st dec. row: * P.8, p.2 tog., rep. from * to last 3 sts., p.3. Rep. patt. row, purl 1 row. Change colour and knit 2 rows, change colour and knit 1 row.
2nd dec. row: * P.7, p.2 tog., rep. from * to last 3 sts., p.3. Rep. patt. row, purl 1 row, change colour and knit 2 rows, change colour and knit 1 row.
3rd dec. row: * P.6, p.2 tog., rep. from * to last 3 sts., p.3. Rep. patt. row, purl 1 row, change colour and knit 2 rows, change colour and knit 1 row. Cont. to keep patt. correct and dec. in the same way, working 1 stitch less between decreases until row * P.1, p.2 tog., rep. from * to end has been worked. Rep. patt. row, purl 1 row, change colour and knit 1 row. Change colour. K.2 tog. to end of row. Next 2 rows, K.2 tog. to last st., k.1. Break wool, draw through rem. sts., secure firmly. Press lightly and join seam. Press seam. Trim with long tassel of remaining wool.

Striped cap with bobble

Football fan, rally driver, or student, for fishing, sailing or ski-ing, this is the cap so many people need, be they boy or girl

Materials: 2 ozs. Sirdar Double Knitting Wool in main colour and oddments in 3 contrasting colours; a pair of No. 8(5) knitting needles.

Tension: 6½ sts. and 8 rows to 1 inch over pattern.

Measurements: To fit an average head.

Abbreviations: See Page 10

TO MAKE
With Main colour, cast on 142 sts.
1st row: P.1, * k.2, p.1, rep. from * to end. 2nd row: K.1, * p.2, k.1, rep. from * to end. **3rd row:** As 1st.
4th row: K. These 4 rows form the patt. Repeat them twice more. Change to first contrast and k.1 row. Beg. with 2nd row, work 7 rows of patt. Change to 2nd contrast and knit 1 row. Beg. with 2nd row, work 3 rows patt. Change to 3rd contrast and k. 1 row. Work 2nd patt. row. Change to main colour and k. 1 row. Cont. in patt. until work measures 5 ins. from beg. ending with a 4th row. Keeping patt. correct, **Shape Top:**
Next row: * Patt. 8, k.2 tog., rep. from * to last 2 sts. patt. 2. Next and every alt. row. Work to end.
Next row: * Patt. 7, k.2 tog., rep. from * to end.
Next dec. row: * Patt. 6, k.2 tog., rep. from * to end. Cont. to dec. on alt. rows in this way until 30 sts. remain.
Next row: K.2 tog., to end. Draw wool through rem. sts. and secure. Join seam. Trim top with pompon.

Stocking cap

Just a long straight piece of plain knitting with a tassel on the end. Arrange to suit yourself and the rest makes a scarf. You will find more than one way to wear it. Have fun trying

Materials: 5 ozs. Sirdar Talisman 4-ply in Peacock blue; 3 ozs. in Turquoise; 2 ozs. in orange and 1 in white;
a pair of No. 9(4) knitting needles.

Tension: $6\frac{1}{2}$ sts. and $8\frac{1}{2}$ rows to 1 inch.

Measurements: To fit an average head; Length: approx. 60 ins.

Abbreviations: See page 10

TO MAKE
With Peacock, cast on 130 sts. and work in st.st. throughout. Work 28 rows. Now work in stripes as follows. * 6 rows turquoise, 2 rows white, 6 rows turquoise, 14 rows peacock, 6 rows orange, 2 white, 6 rows orange, 14 rows peacock. * Rep. from * to * until piece measures 60 ins. Cast off. Press lightly. Fold in half lengthwise, and join long seam neatly. Turn to right side and press with seam in centre of one side. Fold cast on edge to last row of 28 peacock rows and catch down. Gather cast off edge and secure firmly. Cut remaining wool into 4 inch lengths to make a tassel and sew to gathered end of cap.

Aran cap and mitts

for colour illustration see page 26

If you can't face a whole sweater in Aran stitches, go for small accessories like this and enjoy these traditional patterns

Materials: 4 balls of Mahony's Blarney Bainin; a pair each of Nos. 7(6) and 9(4) knitting needles, 2 cable needles.

Tension: 9 sts. and 13 rows to 2 ins. over st.st. on No. 7(6) needles.

Measurements: Cap: to fit an average head; Mitts: Round palm: 7½ ins.; length of hand excluding ribbing: 7½ ins.

Abbreviations: See Page 10

CAP

With No. 9(4) needles, cast on 93 sts., and work 9 rows k.1, p.1 rib. Change to No. 7(6) needles.

Next row: * P. twice into next st., p.1, rep. from * to last st. p. twice into last st. Now cont. in patt.

1st row: P.1, * k.6, (p.2, k.2) 3 times, p.2, rep. from * ending last rep. p.1.

2nd row: K.1, *(p.2, k.2) 3 times, p.6, k.2, rep. from * ending last rep. k.1.

3rd row: P.1, * C3L. C3R., p.2, C6R., p.2, k.2, p.2, rep. from * ending last rep. p.1.

4th row: As 2nd.

5th and 6th rows: As 1st and 2nd.

7th row: P.1, * C3R., C3L., p.2, k.2, p.2, C6L., p.2, rep. from * ending last rep. p.1. **8th row:** As 2nd. Rep. these 8 rows until work measures 5 ins. from beg. ending on wrong side.

Next row: P.1, * patt. 6, p.2 tog., patt. 10, p.2 tog., rep. from * ending last rep. p.1 instead of p.2 tog. Cont. in patt. as set with p.1 instead of p.2 between panels until work measures 6½ ins. from beg. ending on right side.

Next row: P.1, * p.2 tog., p.3, p.2 tog., p.2, rep. from * to end. Cont. in k.1, p.1 rib.

Shape Top: 1st and every alt. row: K.1, p.1, to last st., k.1.

2nd row: Rib 6, * p.3 tog., rib 11, rep. from * to last 9 sts., p.3 tog., rib 6.

4th row: Rib 5, * k.3 tog., rib 9, rep. from * to last 8 sts., k.3 tog., rib 5. Cont. to dec. in this way until

12th row: P.1, * k.3 tog., p.1, rep. from * to end. Break wool, draw through rem. sts., fasten off and secure. Press on wrong side with a warm iron over a damp cloth. Join back seam. Add pompon to top of cap.

MITTS

With No. 9(4) needles cast on 39 sts. and work 2 ins. in k.1, p.1 rib. Change to No. 7(6) needles and p. 1 row, increasing 3 times evenly across row. Cont. working 25 sts. for back of hand in patt. as for last part of cap with p.1 between panels and the rem. sts. in purl for palm thus:

1st row: P.1, k.6, p.1, (k.2, p.2) twice, k.2, p.1, k.6, p.17.

2nd row: K.17, p.6, k.1, (p.2, k.2) twice, p.2, k.1, p.6, k.1.

3rd row: P.1, C3L., C3R., p.1, C6R., p.2, k.2, p.1, C3L., C3R., p.17.

4th row: As 2nd. Cont. in patt. as set until work measures 4½ ins. from beg. ending on wrong side. ★★

Shape Thumb: Next row: Work across 31 sts., turn, cast on 3 sts.

Next row: K.9, turn, cast on 4 sts. Work 14 rows in purl fabric on these sts.

Next row: P.1, (p.2 tog., p.1) 4 times.

Next row: K. **Next row:** P.2 tog., 4 times, p.1. Break wool, draw through rem. sts. and fasten off securely. Join seam to base of thumb. With right side facing, rejoin wool at point of right hand needle and pick up 6 sts. along cast on thumb sts. Work to end of row. Work 3½ ins. on these sts. ending on wrong side.

Next row: K.1, (k.2 tog., k.1) 8 times, p.17. **Next row:** K.

Shape Top: 1st row: P.1, p.2 tog., p.11, p.2 tog., p.2, p.2 tog., p.11, p.2 tog., p.1. **2nd row:** K.

3rd row: P.1, p.2 tog., p.9, p.2 tog., p.2, p.2 tog., p.9, p.2 tog., p.1. Cont. to dec. in this way at each end and at each side of centre 2 sts. on every p. row until 14 sts. rem. ending with a dec. row. Divide sts. on to 2 needles and graft or cast off tog.

Left Hand:

Work ribbing as for right hand then reverse patt. and purl fabric thus:

1st patt. row: P.17, k.6, p.1, (k.2, p.2) twice, k.2, p.1, k.6, p.1. Cont. on sts. as now set to ★★.

Shape Thumb: Next row: P.17, turn and cast on 3 sts.

Next row: K.9, turn and cast on 4 sts. Complete thumb and rest of mitt as for right hand reversing shaping. Press lightly on wrong side with a damp cloth and hot iron. Join side seam. Press seams.

Striped stockings

for colour illustration, see page 27

Maybe too gaudy for some, but choose a bright colour if you prefer or play really safe and use straight stocking shades. Anyway, you will be warm in winter legwise

Materials: 3 balls of Sirdar Top Line Nylon D.K., in Blue; 2 balls in Red and yellow and 1 ball in Mulberry; a set of four double pointed needles No. 11(2)

Tension: 8 sts. to 1 inch

Measurements: Length of leg: 24½ ins. Foot: 9 ins. Both adjustable.

Abbreviations: See Page 10

TO MAKE

With Blue, cast on 86 sts. 28 on 1st and 3rd needles and 30 on 2nd needle. Work in k.1, p.1 rib for 28 rounds. Cut blue and join red. **Next round:** K. Cont. in k.1, p.1 rib for a further 17 rounds.

1st dec. round: S.k.p.o., cont. in rib until 3 sts. rem. at end of round, k.2 tog., p.1.

Note: The last p. stitch is the centre back seam. Cont. in k.1, p.1 rib until 27 rounds of red have been worked. Cut red, join yellow. Knit 1 round. Cont. in rib keeping sts. correct over decreasings until 11 rounds have been worked from last dec. round.

2nd dec. round: S.k.p.o., p.1, k.1 rib until 4 sts. rem. k.1, k.2 tog., p.1. Cont. in rib until 27 rounds in yellow have been worked, still decreasing on every 12th round as before. Cut yellow and join Mulberry. Knit 1 round. Cont. in rib, decreasing on every 12th round and working 27 rounds in rib in each colour. Always work 1 knit round when changing colour. When 58 sts. are left on needles, work without further shaping until 27 rounds in 2nd stripe in Mulberry have been completed. Cut Mulberry. Arrange the sts. from 1st and 3rd needles on one needle, having the p. seam stitch in the centre with 14 sts. on each side. (29 sts.) Divide the instep sts. on two needles. Join Blue to beg. of 29 heel sts. and work 18 rows in st.st.

Turn Heel: K.17, s.k.p.o., k.1, turn.

2nd row: P.9, p.2 tog., p.1, turn.

Fair isle mitts

3rd row: K.10, s.k.p.o., k.1, turn.
4th row: P.11, p.2 tog., p.1, turn.
5th row: K.12, s.k.p.o., k.1, turn.
6th row: P.13, p.2 tog., p.1, turn.
7th row: K.14, s.k.p.o., k.1, turn.
8th row: P.15, p.2 tog., p.1, turn.
9th row: K.16, s.k.p.o., k.1, turn.
10th row: P.19. **11th row:** K.19.

Now pick up and knit 12 sts. from left side of heel flap. With next needle, knit the 29 sts. from instep on to one needle, with next needle, pick up and knit 12 sts. from other side of heel flap. K. 9 sts. from 1st needle on to 3rd needle. (72 sts.) Now begin shaping.

1st round: 1st needle: K. to last 3 sts., k.2 tog., k.1. 2nd needle: K.1, p.1, to last st., k.1. 3rd needle: K.1, s.k.p.o., k. to end.
2nd round: 1st needle: Knit. 2nd needle: K.1, p.1, to last st., k.1. 3rd needle: Knit. Repeat last 2 rounds 6 times more. Now repeat 2nd round only until foot measures 7 ins. changing to Red after 28 rounds and working 18 rounds only in Red. Change to Yellow and work 5 rounds.
Shape Toe: 1st round: 1st needle: K. to last 3 sts., k.2 tog., k.1. 2nd needle: K.1, s.k.p.o., k. to last 3 sts., k.2 tog., k.1. 3rd needle: K.1, s.k.p.o., k. to end.
2nd round: Knit. Repeat last 2 rounds until 22 sts. remain.
Arrange remaining sts. evenly on 2 needles and graft the stitches. Fasten off. Make another stocking to match.

Made plain and decorated after with Swiss darning, see page 13. So easy you can make a pair in an evening. Embroider them to suit your fancy

Materials: 2 ozs. Sirdar Double Knitting Wool in white; scraps of Red, Black and Blue for Swiss darning; a pair of No. 10(3) and 8(5) knitting needles.

Tension: $5\frac{1}{2}$ sts., and $7\frac{1}{2}$ rows to 1 inch over stocking stitch.

Measurements: Length: 10 ins., round hand: 8 ins.

Abbreviations: See Page 10

TO MAKE

With No. 10(3) needles and white wool cast on 40 sts. work 6 rows of k.2, p.2 rib. Change to red and work 6 rows. Change to white and work 12 rows. Change to No. 8(5) needles and st.st. Work 4 rows. Increase 1 st. at end of last row.

Shape for thumb: 1st row: K.20, p.u.k., k.1, p.u.k., k. to end.
2nd and alt. rows: Purl.
3rd row: K.20, p.u.k., k.3, p.u.k., k. to end.
5th row: K.20, p.u.k., k.5, p.u.k., k. to end. Cont. to increase in this way on all knit rows until there are 53 sts. on needle, ending with a p. row.
Thumb: 1st row: K.33, turn. **2nd row:** P.13, turn and cast on 2 sts.
3rd row: K.15. **4th row:** P.15. Repeat these 2 rows twice more.
Shape Top of Thumb: K.1, k.2 tog., k. to last 3 sts., k.2 tog., k.1.
Next row: Purl. Repeat these 2 rows twice more. Break wool, thread through remaining sts. and fasten off securely.
Hand: Return to remaining sts. and with right side facing, join wool to sts. on left hand needle. Knit to end.
Next row: P.20, cast on 2 sts., purl across other set of sts. Work 3 ins. in st.st. on these sts.
Shape Top: 1st row: *K.1, k.2 tog., k.15, k.2 tog., k.1, rep. from * to end.
2nd and alt. rows: Purl.
3rd row: * K.1, k.2 tog., k.13, k.2 tog., k.1, rep. from * to end.
5th row: * K.1, k.2 tog., k.11, k.2 tog., k.1, rep. from * to end.
7th row: * K.1, k.2 tog., k.9, k.2 tog., k.1, rep. from * to end. **8th row:** * P.1, p.2 tog., p.7, p.2 tog., p.1, rep. from * to end. Cast off. Make another mitt to match.

TO MAKE UP
Press pieces. Embroider back of each hand with Swiss darning, following chart 2 Begin with 1 row of 1 stitch red, 1 white. next row 1 stitch white, 1 red. Then repeat these 2 rows using black in place of red and repeat them using red again. Continue with diamond pattern on back only. Press on wrong side. Join side and thumb seams. Press seams.

✕ Red
╱ Blue
• Black

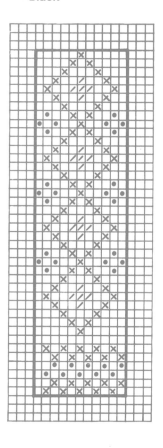

Summer gloves on two needles

Made in cool cotton for the summer, slightly starched for a crisper look. You can forget the frill, make a longer rib and they would make good riding or driving gloves

Materials: 2 balls of Twilley's Stalite; a pair each of Nos. 11(2) and 12(1) knitting needles.

Tension: 7 sts. and 9 rows to 1 inch over st.st.

Measurements: To fit an average hand.

Abbreviations: See page 10

TO MAKE

With No. 11(2) needles, cast on 58 sts., inserting point of right hand needle into each preceeding loop.
1st row: K.1B., * p.2, k.1B., rep. from * to end.
2nd row: P.1, * k.1B., k.1, p.1, rep. from * to end. Repeat these 2 rows 4 times.
Next row: K.1B., * drop next st. off needle, p.1, k.1B., rep. from * to end. (39 sts.) Change to No. 12(1) needles.
1st row: P.1, * k.1B., p.1, rep. from * to end.
2nd row: K.1B., * p.1, k.1B., rep. from * to end. Rep. these 2 rows twice more. Allow the dropped sts. from last row of frill stitch to run down to cast on edge. Change to No. 11(2) needles. Work in pattern and begin to shape the thumb.
1st row: P.2, * p.u.k., p.7, rep. from * to last 2 sts., p.u.k., p.2. (45 sts.)
1st pattern row: K.1, * p.u.k., k.1, slip made st. over knit st., k.1, rep. from * to end. **2nd row:** Purl. These 2 rows form the pattern.
To Shape Thumb: 1st row: Patt. 21 k. twice into next st., k.1, k. twice into next st., patt. 21.
2nd and alt. rows: Purl.
3rd row: Patt. 21, k.5, patt. 21.

5th row: Patt. 21, k. twice into next st., k.3, k. twice into next st., patt. 21.
7th row: Patt. 21, k.7, patt. 21.
8th row: Purl. Cont. to increase in this way, keeping thumb sts. in st. st., until there are 53 sts. on needle, ending with a p. row.
Next row: Patt. 21, k. to last 21 sts., turn and cast on 2 sts. Leave remaining sts. on a stitch holder.
Next row: P.13, turn and cast on 2 sts., leave remaining sts. on a stitch holder.
Next row: Knit.
Next row: Purl. Work 2¼ ins. in patt. on these 15 sts., ending with a p. row.
Shape Top: K.1, * k.2 tog., rep. from * to end. **Next row:** Purl.
Next row: K.2 tog., to end of row. Cut yarn, draw through rem. sts., and fasten off securely. Join seam. With right side of work facing, rejoin yarn to base of thumb. Pick up and knit 5 sts. from base of thumb, then pattern across sts. from 1st stitch holder. **Next row:** Purl. (47 sts.) Rep. patt. rows for 1¾ ins., ending with a p. row.
1st finger: Patt. 29, turn and cast on 1 st. **Next row:** P.12, turn and cast on 1 st.
Next row: K.2, * p.u.k., k.1, slip made st. over the knit st., k.1, rep. from * to last st., k.1. **Next row:** Purl. Rep. these 2 patt. rows for 2½ ins., ending with a patt. row.
Shape Top: * P.1, p.2 tog., rep. from * to last st., p.1. **Next row:** Knit.
Next row: P.2 tog., to last st., p.1. Fasten off and join seam.
2nd finger: With right side facing, join yarn to base of 1st finger, pick up and knit 2 sts. from base, patt. 6 sts., turn and cast on 1 st.
Next row: P.15, turn and cast on 1 st. Work 3 ins. on these sts. in patt. Shape Top and finish as for first finger.
3rd finger: With right side facing, pick up and knit 2 sts. from base of 2nd

finger, patt. 5 sts., turn and cast on 1 st.
Next row: P.13, turn and cast on 1 st.
Work 2½ ins. in patt. on these sts.,
finish as before.
4th finger: With right side facing, pick up 2 sts. from base of 3rd finger. Patt. across sts. on left hand needle, turn and purl across all sts. Work 2 ins. on these sts. and finish as before. Join final seams. Make another glove in the same way.

Fun Fashion

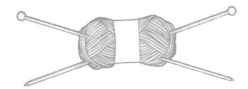

Fashion has always been interesting and never
such fun as it is today. If time is spent knitting
something smart, it must last a little while, so I have
come to terms, just a little, with that fact
of life. If something is fun to wear,
it must quite certainly be comfortable first.
Even if it is eye catching and head turning,
you must be able to put it on and forget about it.
I hope you will like this bright
collection and that the men folk will
enjoy the two included for them

Tartan tabard

for colour illustration, see page 35

Wear it over a cat suit if you have the nerve, but it would look just as good over slacks

Materials: 12 ozs. Sirdar Double Crepe in Black; 7 ozs. in yellow and 6 ozs. in red; a pair each of Nos. 8(5) and 9(4) knitting needles; a stitch holder.

Tension: 15 sts. and 13 rows to 2 ins.

Measurements: To fit Bust 32 to 34 ins. Length: 31 ins.

Abbreviations: See Page 10. Also for this design only Black., A; Yellow., B; Red., C.

TO MAKE
With No. 8(5) needles, and Black cast on 103 sts. Work in st.st. in the foll. tartan pattern.

1st row: * K.1C, 5B, 6A., 2C., 1A., 1C., rep. from * to last 7 sts., 1C., 5B., 1A.
2nd row: * P.2B., 2A., 1B., 2C., 1B., 2A., 2C., 4A., rep. from * to last 7 sts., 2B., 2A., 1B., 2C.
3rd row: * K.1B., 2C., 3A., 2B., 2A., 2C., 2A., 2B., rep. from * to last 7 sts., 1B., 2C., 3A., 1B.
4th row: * P.3A., 2C., 1A., 4B., 2A., 2C., 2B., rep. from * to last 7 sts., 3A., 2C., 1A., 1B.
5th row: * K.3A., 2C., 3A., 2B., 2A., 4B., rep. from * to last 7 sts., 3A., 2C., 2A.
6th row: * P.1A., 2C., 5A., 6B., 2C., rep. from * to last 7 sts., 1A., 2C., 4A.
7th row: * K.5A., 3C., 2A., 4B., 2A., rep. from * to last 7 sts., 5A., 2C.
8th row: * P.2C., 8A., 4B., 1A., 1C., rep. from * to last 7 sts., 2C., 5A.
9th row: * K.4A., 2C., 1A., 2C., 5B., 2A., rep. from * to last 7 sts., 4A., 2C., 1A.
10th row: * P.2A., 2C., 4A., 2B., 2A., 1B., 2C., 1B., rep. from * to last 7 sts., 2A., 2C., 3A.
11th row: * K.2A., 2C., 2A., 3B., 2C., 3A., 2B., rep. from * to last 7 sts., 2A., 2C., 2A., 1B.
12th row: * P.2B., 2A., 2C., 2B., 3A., 2C., 1A., 2B., rep. from * to last 7 sts., 2B., 2A., 2C., 1B.
13th row: * K.2B., 2A., 4B., 3A., 2C., 3A., rep. from * to last 7 sts., 2B., 2A., 3B.
14th row: * P.6B., 2C., 1A., 2C., 5A., rep. from * to last 7 sts., 6B., 1C.
15th row: * K.2A., 4B., 7A., 3C., rep. from * to last 7 sts., 2A., 4B., 1A.
16th row: * P.2A., 4B., 1A., 3C., 6A., rep. from * to last 7 sts., 2A., 4B., 1A.
These 16 rows form the pattern and are repeated. Cont. straight until work measures 27 ins. from beg., ending with a p. row. **Next row:** K.29, place rem. sts. on stitch holder.

Shape Neck: Cast off 3 sts. at beg. of next row and cont. to cast off 3 more sts. at this edge once more. Work straight on rem. 23 sts. until measurement is 30 ins. from beg., ending with a k. row. Place these sts. on a spare needle and return to rem. sts. Join wool to centre edge. Cast off first 45 sts. then work on rem. sts. to match other side, ending with same patt. row as other shoulder.
Next row: P.23, cast on 57 sts. for back of neck, p. across rem. 23 sts. from spare needle. Cont. straight on all sts. until measurement is 29 ins. from cast on sts. at back of neck. Cast off.

Border: With No. 9(4) needles, and Black, cast on 13 sts.
1st row: K.2 tog., k. to last st., k. twice into this st.
2nd row: P. Repeat these 2 rows until border is long enough to fit all round edge of tabard. Cast off. Make a similar bias binding to go round neck.

TO MAKE UP
Press on wrong side with a hot iron over a damp cloth. Back stitch the bias binding all round tabard, fold inside in half, to wrong side of work and catch into place. Sew binding to neck in same way. Press edges.

Man's aran jerkin

for colour illustration, see page 39

For the man who likes something with a bit of style. Super Aran stitches make a jerkin to wear with flair

Materials: 11(12,13) balls of Mahony's Blarney Bainin;
an extra ball if belt is made;
a pair each of Nos. 7(6) and 9(4) knitting needles;
2 cable needles;
6 buttons;
a buckle for belt;
1½ yds. of 1½ inch facing ribbon.

Tension: 5 sts. and 6½ rows to 1 inch over double moss stitch.

Measurements: Chest: 38(41,44) ins.
Length: 28½ ins.

Abbreviations: See Page 10

BACK

With No. 9(4) needles, cast on 115(123, 131) sts. and work 2 rows k.1, p.1 rib. Change to No. 7(6) needles and purl 1 row. Now cont. in patt.

1st row: (K.1, p.1) 4(4,6) times, k.1, * p.2(3,3), k.b.1., p.2(3,3), T2F., p.5, cable 5, p.5, T2B., p.2(3,3), k.b.1., p.2 (3,3)*, T2F., p.1, k.9, p.1, T2B., p.1, (k.1, p.1) 3 times, k.1, p.1, T2F., p.1, k.9, p.1, T2B., rep. from * to *, (k.1, p.1), 4(4,6) times, k.1.

2nd row: (P.1, k.1) 4(4,6) times, p.1, *k.2(3,3), p.b.1, k.2(3,3), p.2, k.5, p.2, k.1, p.2, k.5, p.2, k.2(3,3), p.b.1., k.2(3,3), * p.2, k.1, p.9, k.1, p.2, k.1, (p.1, k.1) 3 times, p.1, k.1, p.2, k.1, p.9, k.1, p.2, rep. from * to *(p.1, k.1) 4(4,6) times, p.1.

3rd row: (P.1, k.1) 4(4,6) times, p.1, * p.2(3,3), k.b.1, p.2(3,3), T2F., p.4, C3R., k.1, C3L., p.4, T2B., p.2(3,3), k.b.1., p.2(3,3), * T2F., p.1, DC9., p.1, T2B., p.1, (p.1, k.1) 3 times, p.1, (for double moss stitch), p.1, T2F., p.1, DC9., p.1, T2B., rep. from * to *, (p.1, k.1) 4(4,6) times, p.1.

4th row: (K.1, p.1) 4(4,6) times, k.1, * k.2(3,3), p.b.1., k.2(3,3), p.2, k.4, p.2, k.1, p.1, k.1, p.2, k.4, p.2, k.2(3,3), p.b.1, k.2(3,3) *, p.2, k.1, p.9, k.1, p.2, k.1, (k.1, p.1) 3 times, k.1, (for double moss stitch), k.1, p.2, k.1, p.9, k.1, p.2, rep. from * to *, (k.1, p.1) 4(4,6) times, k.1.
These 4 rows complete the patt. of the twisted rib, lobster claw and double moss stitch panels. Keeping these correct, cont. on the diamond panels of 15 sts. thus:-

5th row: P.3, C3R., k.1, p.1, k.1, C3L., p.3.
6th row: K.3, p.2, (k.1, p.1) twice, k.1, p.2, k.3.
7th row: P.2, C3R., d.m.st.5, C3L., p.2.
8th row: K.2, p.2, d.m.st.7, p.2, k.2.
9th row: P.1, C3R., d.m.st.7, C3L., p.1.
10th row: K.1, p.2, d.m.st.9, p.2, k.1.
11th row: P.1, C3L., d.m.st.7, C3R., P.1.
12th row: K.2, p.2, d.m.st. 7, p.2, k.2.
13th row: P.2, C3L., d.m.st.5, C3R., p.2.
14th row: K.3, p.2, d.m.st.5, p.2, k.3.
15th row: P.3, C3L., d.m.st.3, C3R., p.3.
16th row: K.4, p.2, d.m.st.3, p.2, k.4.
17th row: P.4, C3L., p.1, C3R., p.4.
18th row: K.5, p.2, k.1, p.2, k.5.
These 18 rows complete the diamond patt. Beginning again at 1st row of diamond, but noting that the next row will be the 3rd of lobster claw, cont. in patt. until 8 rows of 7th diamond have been worked. **
Shape Armholes: Cast off 5(7,9) sts: at beg. of next 2 rows, then dec. 1 st. at each end of the next 5 rows. Now dec.

1 st. at each end of the next 6(6,7) right side rows. Cont. without further shaping on 83(87,89) sts. with an extra p. st. outside diamond on 3rd size, until 2nd row of 11th diamond has been worked. **Shape Shoulders:** Cast off 7 sts. at beg. of next 4 rows and 8(9,10) sts. on foll. 2 rows. Cast off rem. sts.

LEFT FRONT

With No. 9(4) needles, cast on 63(67,71) sts. and work as for Back to end of ribbing. Purl 1 row. Cont. in patt. as for right hand side of Back but with 9 sts. at front edge in double moss stitch thus:-
1st row: (K.1, p.1) 4(4,6) times, k.1, rep. from * to * of 1st patt. row, T2F., p.1, k.9, p.1, T2B., p.1, (k.1, p.1) 4 times, k.1. Cont. in patt. as set for 5 more rows.
Next row: Work to last 7 sts., cast off 3, double moss stitch to end. In next row, cast on sts. over those cast off in previous row. Cont. in patt. for 28 rows, then make another buttonhole in next 2 rows. Make 5 more buttonholes with 28 rows between and cont. until work matches Back to **.
Shape Armhole: Cast off 5(7,9) sts. at beg. of next row then dec. 1 st. at same edge on every row 5 times. Then on right side rows only 6(6,7) times. Cont. without further shaping on 47(49,50) sts. until the 16th row of the 9th diamond has been worked. (2 rows after last buttonhole)
Shape Neck: Next row: Patt. 22(23, 24), turn. Leave rem. sts. on spare needle and cont. in patt. until 2nd row of 11th diamond has been worked.
Shape Shoulder: Cast off 7 sts. at beg. of next 2 rows beg. at armhole edge, then 8(9,10) sts. at same edge on next row.

RIGHT FRONT

Work to match Left Front reversing front border thus:
1st patt. row: (K.1, p.1) 4 times, k.1, p.1, T2F., p.1, k.9, p.1, T2B., rep. from * to* of 1st patt. row of Back, (k.1, p.1) .. 4(4,6) times, k.1. Cont. to match with Left Front, omitting buttonholes and working an extra row to end at side edge before shaping armhole, until 16th row of 9th diamond has been worked.
Shape Neck: With No. 9(4) needle, k.25 (26,26) and leave on spare needle. Change to No. 7(6) needles and cont. to match Left Front, but working 1 extra row before shaping shoulder.

NECK AND ARMHOLE BORDERS

Pin out and press on wrong side with hot iron and a damp cloth. Join shoulders. Slip the sts. of Right Front neck on to a No. 9(4) needle, then on to the same needle, pick up and knit 21 sts. up side of neck, 39(41,41) sts. across Back of Neck, 21 sts. down other side of neck and k. sts. from spare needle. Work 2 rows k.1, p.1 rib. Cast off in rib, taking 2 tog., each side of each front corner while casting off. Work armhole borders to match, picking up and knitting 123(127,131) sts. round each armhole and working 4 rows in rib.

BELT

With No. 9(4) needles, cast on 13 sts.
1st row: Sl.1, (k.1, p.1) to last 2 sts., k.2.
2nd row: Sl.1, (p.1, k.1) to end. Rep. these 2 rows for required length, ending with 2nd row. Now dec. 1 st. at each end of every row until 3 sts. remain. P.3 tog., fasten off.

TO MAKE UP

Join side seams. Face front borders with ribbon, cutting and neatening buttonholes. Sew on buttons. Add buckle to belt. Make 2 crochet chain loops and add to sides of jerkin to hold belt. Make another to slip over belt. Press seams.

Blue and yellow pinafore dress

for colour illustration, see page 42

Checked in two colours to wear over shirts or sweaters. The matching sweater on page 60 uses one of the colours only

Materials: Dress: 9(10,11) ozs., yellow and 6(7,8) ozs. blue Wendy 4-ply Nylonised; 3 ozs. Blue Wendy D.K. Nylonised;
a pair each of Nos. 10(3) and 11(2) knitting needles;
a No. 4.00 m.m crochet hook;
a belt buckle.
Sweater: 14(15,16) ozs. Yellow 4 ply. Nylonised.

Tension: 7½ sts. and 11 rows to 1 inch over pattern.

Measurements: Bust: 34(36,38); Hips: 36(38,40) ins.
Dress length: 36 ins., plus fringe;
Sweater length: 24 ins.; Sleeve seam: 17½ ins.

Abbreviations: See Page 10

DRESS BACK
With No. 11(2) needles and yellow, cast on 149(157,165) sts. and beg. with a k. row, work 8 rows st.st. Join on Blue K.2 rows. Change to No. 10(3) needles and beg. patt.
1st row: K. **2nd row:** P. Change to yellow.
3rd and 5th rows: * Sl.1 purlwise, k.3, rep. from * to last st., sl.1 purlwise.
4th and 6th rows: * Sl.1, p.3 yellow, rep. from * to last st., sl.1. Change to Blue. K. 1 row then p. 1 row.
9th and 11th rows: Change to yellow. K.2 yellow, * sl.1 purlwise, k.3 yellow, rep. from * to last 3 sts., sl.1 purlwise, k.2. yellow
10th and 12th rows: P.2 yellow, * sl.1, p.3, yellow, rep. from * to last 3 sts., sl.1, p.2. yellow. These 12 rows form the

pattern and are repeated throughout. Cont. in patt. until Back measures 3 ins. from hemline. Now dec. 1 st. at each end of next and every foll. 10th row until 131(139,147) sts. rem. Then dec. at each end of every foll. 8th row until 101 (109,117) sts. are on needle. (Waist) Now inc. 1 st. at each end of every foll. 6th row until there are 125(133,141) sts. on needle. When Back measures 27 ins. from beg.
Shape Armholes: With right side facing, cast off 7(8,9) sts. at beg. of next 2 rows. Then k.2 tog., at each end of next and every alt. row until 97(103,109) sts. remain. Cont without further shaping until Back measures 36 ins. from hemline.
Shape Shoulders: Cast off 7(7,9) sts. at beg. of next 2 rows and 7(8,8) sts. at beg. of foll. 4 rows. Leave rem. sts. on a spare needle.

FRONT
Work as for Back until waist is reached, then inc. as for Back until there are 121(129,137) sts. on needle.
Divide for centre neck: Work to centre st., cast off centre stitch, turn and complete this side first.
Cont. to inc. at side edge as before until 12 increasings have been completed. Work without further shaping at this edge and dec. 1 st. at neck edge on every 4th row. When work measures the same as Back to armhole, ending at side edge, beg. shaping.
Shape Armholes: Cast off 7(8,9) sts. at beg. of next row. Then k.2 tog., at armhole edge on alt. rows 7 times.
At the same time, cont. to dec. at neck edge as before until 21(23,25) sts. rem. ending at side edge.
Shape Shoulders: Cast off 7(7,9) sts. at beg. of next row and 7(8,8) at beg. of foll. 2 alt. rows.

40

Poncho in squares

for colour illustration, see page 2

Rejoin yarn to centre and work to match other side.

Press work carefully.

Join left shoulder seam and press. With No. 11(2) needles and blue, cast on 60(62,64) sts. With right side facing, pick up and knit 70(72,74) sts. from right side of V-neck. Beg. with a p. row, work 3 rows st.st., purl 2 rows and work 2 rows st.st. Cast off loosely.

With right side facing and No. 11(2) needles, pick up and knit 125(129,133) sts. from back of neck and left side of V-neck. Work to match other half. Join right shoulder seam and press. Turn neck facing to wrong side on purl hemline and slip stitch. Join edges of crossover binding very neatly and catch down to form mock crossover.

Armhole Binding: With Blue and No. 11(2) needles, pick up and knit 148 sts. round armhole. Work as for front facing.

TO MAKE UP

Join side seams. Turn in and slip stitch armhole facings. Press seams. Turn up hem.

Fringe: With crochet hook and D.K. yarn join to side edge of lower edge through blue line at hem edge. Make 42 chain, work 1 double crochet into 3rd k. st. along hem. Cont. in this way all round hemline. Fasten off.

Belt: With Blue and No. 10(3) needles, and D.K. yarn, cast on 8 sts. and work 30 ins. in g. st. Cast off. Add buckle. Make belt loops in crochet chain and add to waist line at side edges.

If you can knit a square you can make this gay poncho. As easy as pie and all you need will be odd ounces and as many colours as you like to use

The Poncho takes 24 squares, made in the same way and to the same tension as those for the bedspread on page 113. It measures 25 inches square, excluding the fringe.

TO MAKE

Make 4 strips each with 5 squares and join the remaining 4 squares together in pairs.

Join two strips of five squares matching corners carefully, then join a pair of two squares to each side of one edge, leaving one square free in the centre. Join the other two strips of five squares together in the same way and add to the other side of the centre pairs, still leaving a free square in the centre for neck. With right side facing, with No. 9(4) needles, pick up and knit across one edge of neck. Work 4 rows k.1, p.1 rib, decreasing 1 st. at each end on 2nd and 4th rows. Cast off in rib. Work other three sides to match. Join corners of neck ribbing. Press Poncho on wrong side. Add fringes all round lower edge.

Long skirt and shawl

for colour illustration, see page 43

You'll never be cold shouldered in this brightly striped shawl, with the skirt added it makes a gorgeously warm set for evenings at home

Materials: 18(18,19) balls of Wendy Tricel/Nylon D.K. in main colour and 5 balls in first contrast and 3 in 2nd; a No. 7(6) and 8(5) circular needle 30 ins. long and a No. 9(4) circular needle 24 inches long;
waist length of elastic for skirt.
For shawl: 12 balls of 1st; 5 balls 2nd and 3 balls 3rd contrast.

Tension: 6 sts. and 7 rows to 1 inch, on No. 7(6) needles.

Measurements: Waist: 26(28,30) ins. Hip: 36(38,40) ins.; Length of skirt: 40 ins.

Abbreviations: See page 10

Note on shawl: As shaping is worked by turning before the end of every row, always knit into the back of last st., before turning and slip first st., pulling yarn tight to avoid holes.

SHAWL

With No. 9(4) circular needle and 1st colour, cast on 480 sts. Knit 1 row.
2nd row: K.479, turn. **3rd row:** k.478, turn. Beg. shaping. **1st row:** K.237, sl.1, k.1, p.s.s.o., k.2 tog., k.236, turn. **2nd row:** Sl.1, p.473, turn. **3rd row:** K.235, sl.1, k.1, p.s.s.o., k.2 tog., k.234, turn. **4th row:** Sl.1, p.469, turn. Cont. to work in this way, decreasing 2 sts. at centre of every k. row and leaving 1 stitch extra at end of every row until 24 rows have been completed. Change to 2nd colour and work 16 rows in same way. Change to 3rd colour and work 2 rows, then 2 rows 2nd colour, 2 rows 3rd, 2 rows 2nd, 12 rows 3rd. Change to 1st colour and repeat the striped sequence but leaving 2 sts. less on every row. Change to 1st colour and cont. in this leaving 3 sts. less on every row. Last 2 rows will be worked thus: Sl.1, sl.1, k.1, p.s.s.o., k.2 tog., turn. **Next row:** Sl.1, p.1, turn. Break yarn and slip sts. from right hand needle on to left hand. With No. 8(5) circular needle, and 1st colour, knit into back of all sts. across all sts. Work 3 rows in g.st. Cast off with No. 7(6) needle.
Trim pointed edge with fringe.

SKIRT

With No. 7(6) needle, cast on 384 sts. with first colour. Work 4 rows g.st. Join into ring and begin chevrons.
1st round: * K.1, k.2 tog., k.13, p.u.k., and knit into back of it, k.1, p.u.k., k.13, sl.1, k.1, p.s.s.o., rep. from * to end.
2nd round: K. These 2 rounds form the chevron. When 24 rounds have been worked, change to 2nd colour and work 16 rounds. Change to 3rd colour and work 2 rounds, then 2 rounds 2nd, 2 rounds 3rd, 2 rounds 2nd, and 12 rounds 3rd. Change to No. 8(5) needles and repeat these stripes once, beg. with 1st colour. Change to No. 9(4) needles and 1st colour again

Red fringed dress

for colour illustration, see page 47

and work 4 rounds. This completes
chevron patt. Still with 1st colour,
Begin shaping:
Next round: K.14, * sl.1, k.1, p.s.s.o.,
k.1, k.2 tog., k.27, rep. from * ending
last rep. with sl.1, k.1, p.s.s.o., k.1, k.2
tog., k.13. Now work 14(17,20) rounds in
st.st., (Every round K.)
Next round: K.13, * sl.1, k.1, p.s.s.o.,
k.1, k.2 tog., k.25, rep. from * ending
last rep. sl.1, k.1, p.s.s.o., k.1, k.2 tog.,
k.12. Work 14(17,20) rounds st.st.
Work 2 further dec. rounds on next and
foll. 15th(18th, 21st) rounds. Then on
19th(23rd, 25th) rounds., until 9(8,7)
decreases in all have been worked. There
will be 2 sts. less between decs. on each
succeeding round. Cont. without further
shaping until skirt measures 40 ins., or
desired length from point of chevron.
Cast off.

TO MAKE UP
Join side edges. Join waist elastic into a
ring and set to waist on wrong side with
casing stitch.

Tailored to fit with slimming darts.
The fringes add the final touch to a
very plain dress which you will find
easy to make

Materials: 31(33,35) ozs. Wendy
Double Knitting Nylonised and three
50 gramme balls of Wendy Diabolo
Double Double Knitting to match;
1 pair each of Nos. 9(4) and 10(3) knitting
needles;
a 22 inch zip fastener;
a medium sized crochet hook.

Tension: 6 sts. and 8 rows to 1 inch on
No. 9(4) needles.

Measurements: Bust: 34(36, 38) ins.
Hip' 36(38,40) ins. Length: 41(41¼,
41½) ins. Sleeve:17 ins.

Abbreviations: See Page 10

THE DRESS
Worked in 1 piece to the armholes.
With No. 9(4) needles and D.K., cast
on 272(284,296) sts. and work 6 rows
k.1, p.1 rib, knitting into back of all k.
sts. on right side rows.
Next row: K.5, p.1, k. to last 6 sts.,
p.1, k.5. **Next row:** P. Rep. last 2 rows
10 times more.
Next row: K.5, p.1, k.28(30,32), * k.2
tog., k.1, (mark the last st.) sl.1, k.1,
p.s.s.o., * k.61(63,65), rep. from * to *
k.62(66,70), rep. from * to * k.61(63,65),
rep. from * to *, k.28(30,32), rep. from
* to *, p.1, k.5. Keeping the 2 p. sts. in
line, work 21 rows. **Next row:** Dec. at
each side of the marked sts. as for first
row. Cont. to decrease, working 19 rows
between each set of decreasing until
224(236,248) sts. remain.
Cast off 3 sts. at beg. of next 2 rows. Work
11 rows, then dec. as before. Work 13
rows between each of the next 2 dec. rows.

45

Work 7 rows between each of the next 2 dec. rows. Work 5 rows between each dec. row until 154(166,178) sts. rem. Work 9 rows straight.

Now make 1 at each side of marked sts. on next and every foll. 4th row until there are 210(222,234) sts. remaining. Cont. without further shaping until work measures 8 ins. from the beginning of the increase, ending after a p. row.

Divide for Armholes: Next row:
Work 48(50,52) sts., cast off 9(11,13), k.96(100,104), cast off 9(11,13), work 48(50,52). Working on the last set of sts., dec. 1 st. at armhole edge on next 7 rows. Cont. without further shaping until armhole measures 5($5\frac{1}{4}$,$5\frac{1}{2}$) ins., ending at front edge.

Shape Neck: Cast off 5(6,7) sts. at beg. of next row, then dec. 1 st. on every row at the neck edge until 23(24,25) sts. remain. Cont. without further shaping until armhole measures 6$\frac{3}{4}$(7,7$\frac{1}{4}$) ins., ending at shoulder edge.

Shape Shoulder: Cast off 7(8,8) sts. at beg. of next row, then cast off 8 sts. at beg. of next alt. row then, 8(8,9) sts. at beg. of foll. alt. row. Return to centre sts. and work Back. Dec. 1 st. at each end of next 7 k. rows. Cont. without further shaping until armhole measures the same as the front. Shape shoulders to match front, then cast off remaining sts.

SLEEVES

With No. 10(3) needles, cast on 44 (48,52) sts. and work 2$\frac{1}{2}$ ins. in twisted rib. Change to No. 9(4) needles and st.st. Inc. 1 st. at each end of next and every foll. 6th row until there are 80(84,88) sts. on needle. Cont. straight until sleeve measures 17 ins. from beg., ending with a p. row.

Shape Top: Cast off 5(6,7) sts. at beg. of next 2 rows, then dec. 1 st. at each end of next 12(8,4) rows. Now dec. 1 st. at each end of next and every foll. alt. row until 38 sts. remain.

Dec. 1 st. at each end of next 4 rows. Cast

off 3 sts. at beg. of next 4 rows. Cast off rem. sts.

Front Borders:
With right side of work facing and with No. 10(3) needles, pick up and knit 234(236,238) sts. along line of p. sts. at front edge. Work 4 rows in twisted rib. Cast off in rib. Work other side to match.

Neckband:
With right side facing and No. 10(3) needles, pick up and knit 108(110,112) sts. round neck. Work 3 ins. twisted rib. Cast off in rib.

Pockets:
Cast on 39(41,43) sts. and beg. with a p. row work 15 rows in st. st.

Next row: K.17(18,19), k.2 tog., k.1, (mark the last st.) sl.1, k.1, p.s.s.o., k.17(18,19). Work 5 rows. Rep. last 6 rows and dec. on each side of marked st. 3 times more. Work 4 rows. Beg. with a k. row to reverse work, work 4 more rows. Now inc. 1 st. at each side of marked st. Work 5 rows. Cast off. Make another pocket to match.

Fringes:
Using Diabolo double and with crochet hook, make 19 chain. Change to single yarn and make 24 chain. *Slip stitch into first of the 24 sts. and last of double yarn chain. Slip stitch into next double yarn chain, make 24 chain and repeat from *
* to end. Make two for wrists.

For pockets, work in same way using 13 chain in double yarn as base. For Shoulders work on a base of 21 double yarn chain.

TO MAKE UP

Press pieces. Turn hem of pockets to wrong side and catch down. Sew fringes to edges of pockets. Turn neck band in half to wrong side and catch down. Set zip into front edges, beg. at top, then join centre seam to bottom of hem. Join shoulder and sleeve seams and set in sleeves. Add fringes to shoulders, wrists and side of sleeves. Add pockets to fronts. Press sleeve and shoulder seams.

Battle blouse and pants

for colour illustration, see page 51

The top is a useful and fashionable little item on its own and with the pants added becomes a smart set

Materials: 19(21,22) balls of Wendy Invitation crochet cotton;
a pair of No. 11(2) knitting needles and a No. 11(2) circular needle;
7 buttons;
1 yd. of 2 inch ribbon for belt backing;
a 10 inch zip fastener. 1 press fastener.

Tension: $7\frac{1}{2}$ sts. and $9\frac{1}{2}$ rows to 1 inch.

Measurements: Blouse: Bust: 32 (34, 36) ins.; Length: centre back $16\frac{1}{2}(17\frac{1}{2}, 18\frac{1}{2})$ ins.; Sleeve seam: $4\frac{1}{2}(5,5)$ ins.
Shorts: Hips: 34(36,38) ins.

Abbreviations: See Page 10

BLOUSE-BACK

With pair of No. 11(2) needles, cast on 110(118,126) sts. and work in st.st. for 4 rows.
Inc. Row: K.26(30,34), p.u.k., knit to last 26(30,34) sts., p.u.k., knit to end. Beg. with a p. row, work 3 rows st.st. Rep. last 4 rows 7 times more. Cont. on these sts. until work measures $7\frac{1}{2}(8, 8\frac{1}{2})$ ins. from beg., ending with a p. row.
Shape Armholes: Cast off 7(8,9) sts. at beg. of next 2 rows, then dec. 1 st. at beg. of next 8 rows. Work without further shaping on these sts. until Armhole measures $6\frac{1}{2}(7, 7\frac{1}{2})$ ins., ending with a p. row.
Shape Shoulders: Cast off 11(12, 13) sts. at beg. of next 4 rows, then cast off 12 sts. at beg. of next 2 rows. Cast off rem. sts.

RIGHT FRONT

With pair of No. 11(2) needles, cast on 64(68, 72) sts. and knit 1 row.
2nd row: P. to last 10 sts., k.10. Rep. last 2 rows once more. **5th row:** K. to last 30 sts., p.u.k., knit to end. **6th row:** As 2nd. **7th row:** As 1st. **8th row:** As 2nd. Rep. last 4 rows until 15(17,19) rows have been worked from beg.
Next row: Make buttonhole: P. to last 10 sts., k.3, cast off 4, k.3.
Next row: K.3, cast on 4, k.3, knit to end. **For 3rd size only,** work p.u.k., on this row as before. Cont. to work p.u.k., increasings on every 4th row until the

8th inc. row has been worked and make 4 more buttonholes working 20(22,24) rows between each. Cont. without further shaping on these sts. until work measures $7\frac{1}{2}(8, 8\frac{1}{2})$ ins. from beg. ending with a K. row.

Shape Armhole: Cast off 7(8,9) sts. at beg. of next row, then dec. 1 st. at same edge on next 4 p. rows. Cont. without further shaping until 5th buttonhole has been worked. Work 5 rows straight, ending at neck edge.

Shape Neck: 1st row: Cast off 21 sts. k. to end. **2nd row:** P. **3rd row:** Dec. 1 st. k. to end. Rep. last 2 rows until 34(36, 38) sts. rem. Work 2 rows, ending at armhole edge.

Shape Shoulders: 1st row: Cast off 11(12,13) sts. work to end. Work 1 row. Rep. last 2 rows. Cast off rem. sts.

LEFT FRONT

Work to match right front, omitting buttonholes and reversing all shapings.

SLEEVES

With pair of No. 11(2) needles, cast on 72(78,84) sts. and work in g.st. for 10 rows. Now change to st.st. for 4(6,8) rows. Inc. 1 st. at each end of next and every 6th row until there are 82(88,94) sts. on needle. Work 3(5,7) rows straight.

Shape Top: Cast off 7(8,9) sts. at beg. of next 2 rows, then dec. 1 st. at beg. of every row until 40 sts. remain. Cast off 5 sts. at beg. of next 4 rows. Cast off rem sts.

COLLAR

Cast on 36(38,40) sts. and work in g.st. Cast on 5 sts. at beg. of 2nd and foll. 11 rows. Now inc. 1 st. at beg. of every row until there are 124(128,132) sts. on needle. Cast off.

WAISTBAND

Cast on 18 sts. and work 6 rows in g.st.
Next row: K. **Next row:** K.4, p.10, k.4. Rep. last 2 rows until band measures 28(30,32) ins. Make a buttonhole.
1st row: K.7, cast off 4 sts., k. to end.
2nd row: K.4, p.3, cast on 4, p.3, k.4. Rep. 7th and 8th rows 15 times, then rep. 2 buttonhole rows. Rep. 7th and 8th rows twice. Work 5 rows g.st. and cast off.

TO MAKE UP

Press pieces with a warm iron over a damp cloth. Join shoulder, side and sleeve seams. Press seams. Set in sleeves. Join collar to neck edge by the shaped edge, starting and ending at centre of front g.st. borders. Mark the centre between two buttonholes in waistband and pin into position at centre of lower edge of front border. Pin band to lower edge, easing bodice into band and leaving last 16 rows of band to extend beyond edge of left front border. Sew into place. Add buttons to match buttonholes. Back waistband with ribbon and cut buttonholes and neaten by working in buttonhole stitch round, working on front of work.

SHORTS

Cast on 144(152, 160) sts. and work 10 rows in g. st. Cont. in st. st. and inc. 1 st. at each end of next and every 4th row until there are 154(162, 170) sts. on needle. Now inc. at each end of every k. row until there are 158(166, 174) sts. on needle. P. 1 row.

To Shape Legs: Cast off 4 sts. at beg. of next 2 rows. Now dec. 1 st. at each end of next and foll. 6 knit rows. Purl these sts. on to the circular needle and leave. Place a coloured marker on this needle.
Make another leg to match the first. Break cotton and purl these sts. on to the circular needle. 272(288, 304) sts. Work in rows of st. st. Work 2 rows.
1st dec. row: * Sl.1, k.1, p.s.s.o., k. to last 2 sts. before end of first leg, (before coloured marker) k.2 tog. Rep. from * on next leg. Work 3 rows st. st. and rep. dec. row again. (264, 280, 296) sts.
Cont. in st.st. until work measures 6½ (7,7½) ins. from beg.
Dart Shaping: * K.40(44,48), k.2 tog., k.48, sl.1, k.1, p.s.s.o., k.40(44,48). Place a coloured marker and work from * once more. Work 5 rows st.st.
2nd dec. row: * K.39(43,47), k.2 tog., k.48, sl.1, k.1, p.s.s.o., k.39(43,47) rep. from * once more. Work 5 rows st.st. Cont. to dec. on every 6th row in this way, keeping 48 sts. between the decreasings until 7 decrease rows have been worked. Work 5 rows st.st. (236,252,268) sts. Now shape Back.
1st row: K.18(19,20), k.2 tog., k.13(16, 17,) k.2 tog., k.24(24,26), k.2 tog., k.22 (22,24) sl.1, k.1, p.s.s.o., k.20(24,26), sl.1, k.1, p.s.s.o., k.22(22,22), k.2 tog., k.20(24, 26), k.2 tog., k.22(22,24), sl.1, k.1, p.s.s.o., k.24(24,26), sl.1, k.1, p.s.s.o., k.13(16,17), sl.1, k.1, p.s.s.o., k.18(19,20). Work 5 rows st.st.
7th row: K.17(18,19), k.2 tog., k.12(15, 16), k.2 tog., k.23(23,25), k.2 tog., k.22 (22,24), sl.1, k.1, p.s.s.o., k.19(23,25), sl.1, k.1, p.s.s.o., k.20(20,20), k.2 tog., k.19 (23, 25), k.2 tog., k.22(22,24), sl.1, k.1, p.s.s.o., k.23(23,25), sl.1, k.1, p.s.s.o., k.12 (15,16), sl.1, k.1, p.s.s.o., k.17(18,19). Work 5 rows st.st.
13th row: K.16(17,18), k.2 tog., k.11 (14,15), k.2 tog., k.22(22,24), sl.1, k.1, p.s.s.o.,

twice, k.18(22,24),
k.2 tog., k.18, k.2 tog., k.18(22,24),
k.2 tog., k.22(22,24),
sl.1, k.1, p.s.s.o., k.22(22,24), sl.1, k.1, p.s.s.o., k.11(14,15), sl.1, k.1, p.s.s.o., k.16(17,18). Work 5 rows st.st.
To shape seat: 1st row: K.15(16,17), k.2 tog., k.10(13,14), k.2 tog., k.21(21,23), k.2 tog., k.22(22,24), sl.1, k.1, p.s.s.o., k.14(18,20), turn.
2nd and each alt. row: Sl.1, p. to end.
3rd row: K.80(84,88), turn. **5th row:** K.70(74,78), turn. **7th row:** K.14(15,16), k.2 tog., k.9(12,13), k.2 tog., k.20(20,22), k.2 tog., k.10(10,12), turn. **9th row:** K.47 (51,55) turn. **11th row:** K.37(41,45), turn. **13th row:** K.13(14,15), k.2 tog., k.8(11, 12), k.2 tog., k.3(3,5), turn. There should now be 26(30,34), sts. on needle. **14th row:** Sl.1, purl across all sts.
15th row: Cast off 2 sts., k.82(90,98), sl.1, k.1, p.s.s.o., k.16(16,16), Note: the last set of sts. are the centre front sts. k.2 tog., k.17(21,23), k.2 tog., k.22(22,24), sl.1, k.1, p.s.s.o., k.21(21,23), sl.1, k.1, p.s.s.o., k.10(13,14), sl.1, k.1, p.s.s.o., k.15(16,17).
16th row: P.86(94,102), turn. **Next and each alt. row:** Sl.1, k. to end.
Now continue to work, matching other side, working decreasings over previous decreasings. Cont. until the row P.26(29,33), turn has been worked.
Next row: Sl.1, k. to end.
Next row: Cast on 8 sts. Knit 8 then dec. 20 sts. evenly across row.
Next row: K. to last st., p.u.k., k.1.
Next row: K.1, p.u.k., k. to end. Rep. last 2 rows once more. Rep. 1st row once more, then knit next row. Now dec. at same edge 5 times. Cast off.

TO MAKE UP

Press work on wrong side with a warm iron over a damp cloth. Join leg seams. Set zip fastener into back seam, beg. below waist band. Join remaining centre seam. Sew press fastener to waistband.

Man's longline sweater

for colour illustration, see page 54

Random yarn makes an interesting sweater for the man who likes a classic. With a wide leather belt it will please the less conventional dresser

Materials: 14(15,16) 50 gramme balls of Patons Double Knitting Wool; a pair each of Nos. 12(1), 9(4), and 7(6) knitting needles; a set of 4 double pointed needles No. 10(3); 1 button.

Tension: 16 sts. and 14 rows to 2 ins. measured slightly stretched over rib pattern on No. 7(6) needles.

Measurements: Chest: 38(40,42) ins. Length: 27(27½, 28) ins. Sleeve: 18 ins.

Abbreviations: See page 10

FRONT

With No. 12(1) needles, cast on 161 (169,177) sts. Change to No. 9(4) needles. Work in rib thus:
1st row: (right side) P.1, (k.1 t.b.l., p.1) to end. **2nd row:** K.1, (p.1, k.1 t.b.l.) to end. Rep. these 2 rows throughout. Work until Front measures 4 ins. from beg. Change to No. 7(6) needles. Cont. in patt. until Front measures 17 ins. from beg., ending with wrong side row.
Shape Armholes: Cast off 5 sts. at beg. of next 4 rows, then dec. 1 st. at each end of next 7(9,11) rows and then of foll. 3 alt. rows. Cont. without further shaping until Front measures 7(7½,8) ins. from beg. of armhole shaping, ending with a wrong side row.
Shape Neck: Rib 44(46,48) turn. Work another 17 rows on these sts. for left shoulder, decreasing 1 st. at neck edge on next and foll. alt. rows until 36(38,40) sts. remain.
Shape Shoulder: Cast off 12 sts. at beg. of next and foll. alt. row then 12(14,16)

sts. at beg. of next alt. row. Slip centre 33 sts. on to a spare needle. Rejoin yarn to remaining sts. and complete to match first side, reversing shapings.

BACK

Work as for Front, omitting front division for neck and working straight after completion of armhole shaping. When Back measures the same as Front to beg. of Shoulder shaping, cast off 12 sts. at beg. of next 4 rows and 12(14,16) sts. at beg. of foll. 2 rows. Leave remaining sts. on a spare needle.

SLEEVES

With No. 9(4) needles, cast on 54(56,58) sts. and work in rib patt. as for main part. When Sleeve measures 3 ins., inc. 27(29,31) sts. evenly across next row. Change to No. 7(6) needles. Inc. 1 st. at each end of every 4th row until there are 125(133,137) sts. Cont. without further shaping until sleeve measures 18 ins.
Shape Top: Cast off 5 sts. at beg. of next 4 rows, then 2 sts. at beg. of foll. 28(30,30) rows. Now cast off 4 sts. at beg. of next 2 rows. Cast off rem. sts.

NECKBAND

Join shoulder seams. With right side facing and set of double pointed needles, rejoin yarn and leaving first 16 sts. on spare needle at front, knit across remaining 17 sts. Cont. to pick up and knit sts. round neck, including 16 sts. from spare needle. Turn and cast on 10 sts. Work 3 rows in twisted rib pattern.
Next row: (Buttonhole row) Patt. to last 7 sts., y.r.n., twice, k.2 tog., patt. to end. Rib 3 more rows, dropping extra loop at buttonhole on next row. Cast off in rib.

TO MAKE UP

Do not press. Join side and sleeve seams. Set in sleeves. Sew button to neckband at side front, to match buttonhole.

Rainbow striped shortie

for colour illustration, see page 55

Make it in rainbow colours for effect or choose the prettiest colours from your odd ounce box

Materials: 2 ozs. Lister Lavenda 4-ply in Main (1st) colour and 1 oz. each in 4 other colours; a pair each of Nos. 10(3) and 11(2) knitting needles.

Tension: 7 sts. and 9 rows to 1 inch on No. 10(3) needles.

Measurements: Bust: 32(34, 36) ins.; Length: 18(18½, 18½) ins.; Sleeve: 4½ ins.

Abbreviations: See Page 10

BACK AND FRONT ALIKE

With No. 11(2) needles, cast on 98 (104,112) sts. in main (1st) colour and work 10 rows k.1, p.1 rib. Change to No. 10(3) needles and st.st. Work 2 rows in each of the 5 colours, beg. with 2nd colour. Cont. in stripes and inc. 1 st. at each end of every 10th row until there are 112(118,126) sts. on needle. Cont.

without further shaping until 90 rows have been worked, thus ending with the 2nd row in main (1st) colour.

Shape Armholes: Cast off 5(6,7) sts. at beg. of next 2 rows, then dec. 1 st. at each end of next and foll. 2 alt. rows. (96, 100, 106) sts. Cont. in stripes for a further 17 rows, thus ending with 2 rows in 3rd colour.

Shape Neck: K.38(40,42) sts., turn. Leave rem. sts. on a spare needle Dec. 1 st. at neck edge on next and alt. rows until 20(22,24) sts. rem. Cont. until armhole measures 7¾(8,8¼) ins. from beg. of armhole shaping ending at armhole edge.

Shape Shoulder: Cast off 10(11,12) sts. at beg. of next and foll. alt. rows. Return to rem. sts. and slip centre 20(20,22) sts. on to a spare needle. Rejoin wool to remaining sts. and complete to match other side.

SLEEVES

With No. 11(2) needles and main(1st) colour, cast on 88(94,100) sts. and work 10 rows in k.1, p.1 rib. Change to No. 10 (3) needles and st. st. in stripes as for main part. Work 40 rows, thus ending with 2nd row of main(1st) colour.

Shape Top: Cast off 5(6,7) sts. at beg. of next 2 rows. Then cast off 3 sts. at beg. of foll. 4 rows and 2 sts. at beg. of next 4 rows. Now dec. 1 st. at each end of alt. rows until 24 sts. remain. Cast off.

NECKBAND

Press pieces and join one shoulder. With main colour and No. 11(2) needles, and with right side facing, pick up and knit 100(104,108) sts. round neck. Work 8 rows in k.1, p.1 rib. Cast off in rib.

TO MAKE UP

Join second shoulder. Set in sleeves, matching stripes from underarm. Join side and sleeve seams. Press seams.

53

Striped sleeveless shortie

for colour illustration, see page 58

Zig-zag stripes make a cute top for summer days. Apart from the main colour, odd ounces will make the coloured stripes
Materials: 6(6,7,7,8) balls of Twilley's Cortina in White; 1 ball each in Rose, Mulberry, Blue and Purple; a pair each of Nos. 10(3) and 12(1) knitting needles.

Tension: 8 sts. and 10 rows to 1 inch.

Measurements: Bust: 30(32,34,36,38) ins. Length from shoulder: 17(17½,17½, 18,18) ins.

Abbreviations: See Page 10

BACK

With No. 12(1) needles and white, cast on 131(139,147,155,163) sts. and work in k.1, p.1 rib for 7 ins. Change to No. 10(3) needles and work in pattern.

1st row: With Rose, k.2, * p.u.k., k.2, sl.1, k.2 tog., p.s.s.o., k.2, p.u.k., k.1, rep. from * to last st., k.1. **2nd row:** K.1, p. to last st., k.1. **3rd and 4th rows:** With white as 1st and 2nd. **5th and 6th rows:** With Mulberry as 1st and 2nd. **7th and 8th rows:** With White as 1st and 2nd. **9th and 10th rows:** With Blue as 1st and 2nd.
11th and 12th rows: With White as 1st and 2nd.
13th and 14th rows: With Purple as 1st and 2nd.
15th and 16th rows: With White as 1st and 2nd. These 16 rows form the striped pattern sequence. Repeat them until work measures 11 ins. from beg., ending with wrong side.
To Shape Armholes: Cast off 8(9,10, 11,12) sts. at beg. of next 2 rows, then dec. 1 st. at each end of next 10 rows. Now dec. 1 st. at each end of foll. 4(5,6,7,8) alt. rows. Cont. on rem. sts. until work measures 17(17½,17½,18,18) ins. from beg., ending with a wrong side row.

Shape Shoulders and neck: Cast off 7(8,8,9,9) patt. until there are 18(18,20,20, 22) sts. on right hand needle. Turn. Leave rem. sts. on a spare needle.
Next row: K.2 tog., work to end.
Next row: Cast off 7(8,8,9,9) sts., work to last 2 sts., k.2 tog.
Next row: K.2 tog., work to end. Cast off rem. sts. With right side of work facing, join on wool and cast off 37(39,39,41,41) sts. for back of neck, patt. to end.
Next row: Cast off 7(8,8,9,9) work to end. Now complete to match first side.

FRONT
Work as for Back until Front measures 10 rows less than back to armhole, ending with a wrong side row. Divide for U-neck.
Next row: Patt. 52(55,59,62,66) sts., turn. Leave rem. sts. on a spare needle. Dec. 1 st. at neck edge on next 8 rows. Work 1 row straight. Work 2 rows here when completing second side.
Shape Armhole: Cast off 8(9,10,11,12) sts. at beg. of next row, then dec. 1 st. at armhole edge on next 10 rows. Now dec. 1 st. at armhole edge on foll. 4(5,6,7,8) alt. rows. Cont. on rem. sts. until Front measures the same as Back to shoulder, ending at armhole edge.

Shape Shoulder: Cast off 7(8,8,9,9) sts. at beg. of next and foll. alt. row. Work 1 row and cast off rem. sts. With right side of work facing, rejoin wool to inner edge of sts. on spare needle. Cast off next 27(29,29,31,31) sts., patt. to end. Complete to match first side noting the exception.
Borders: With right side of work facing, join on White and with No. 12(1) needle, pick up and knit 45(47,47,49,49) sts. round back of neck. Work 6 rows in g.st. Cast off. With right side of work facing and with White, pick up and knit 64(68,68, 72,72) sts. along left side of front neck, 27(29,29,31,31) from cast off group and 64(68,68,72,72) along right side of front neck. Work 6 rows in g.st., cast off.
Armhole Borders: Join shoulder seams. Pick up and knit 118(126,128,136,138) sts. in same way, round armhole. Work 6 rows g.st. Cast off. Work both armholes to match.

TO MAKE UP
Press work lightly on wrong side with a warm iron and a damp cloth. Join side seams. Press seams.

Pink mohair jumper

for colour illustration, see page 59

Made in a gossamer yarn as light as a
feather and as warm as a kiss. Really
feminine with a fragile look
Materials: 4(5,5,6,6) balls of Twilley's
Mohair in Pink and 1 ball in contrast;
a pair of No. 9(4) knitting needles;
crochet hook No. 2.50 m.m.

Tension: 7½ sts. and 10 rows to 1 in.

Measurements: Bust: 32(34,36,38,40) ins.
Length: 20 ins.

Abbreviations: See Page 10

BACK

With two strands of mohair, cast on
112(120,128,136,144) sts. Change to single
yarn and knitting into back of every st.
work in g.st. Inc. 1 st. at each end of
every 13th row until there are 132(140,
148,156,164) sts. on needle. Cont. straight
until Back measures 13 ins. from beg.
Shape Armholes: Cast off 8(9,10,11,12)
sts. at beg. of next 2 rows. Then dec. 1 st.
at each end of next 14(15,16,17,18) rows.
Work straight until armhole measures
7(7,7,7½,7½) ins. from beg. of shaping.
Shape Shoulders: Cast off 7 sts. at beg.
of next 4 rows. Cast off rem. sts.

FRONT

Work as for Back until Front measure s 4
rows less than Back before armhole
shaping.
Shape Neck: Work across 51(55,59,63,67)
sts., turn and complete this side first.
** Cast off 3 sts. at neck edge on alt. row,
then cast off 2 sts. at this edge on next alt.
row. Then dec. 1 st. at this edge of foll.
10(12,14,16,18) rows. **At the same time,**
when front matches Back to armhole, beg.
armhole shaping.
Armhole Shaping: Cast off 8(9,10,11,12)
sts. at side edge, then dec. at this edge

1 st. on foll. 14(15,16,17,18) rows. Work
straight until armhole matches Back to
shoulder.
Shape Shoulder: Cast off 7 sts. at beg. of
next 2 rows at armhole edge.** Rejoin
yarn at inner edge and cast off centre
30 sts. Work to end. Now work from
** to ** reversing shapings.

THE BRAID

With No. 2.50 crochet hook and single
yarn, make 8 chain, using contrast.
1st row: Miss 1st chain, 1 d.c. into 2nd
chain. Work 1 d.c. into each chain to end.
1 chain, turn.
2nd row: As first row, working last
double crochet into turning chain. 1
chain, turn. Repeat 2nd row 4 times.
7th row: Work as for 2nd row for 3
double crochet. Join in main colour. Work
bobble into 4th st. thus: 3 chain, yarn over
hook, and draw loop through 3 times,
wool over hook and draw through all
loops on hook, 1 chain, 1 slip st. into
same st. Drop main and leave at back of
work, with contrast, work to end of row as
before. Repeat 2nd to 7th rows until braid
fits round armhole edge. Make another
piece to match. Make a strip to fit front
and back neck edges.

TO MAKE UP

Press pieces lightly. Sew braid to neck
and armhole edges. Press seams.

Yellow sweater

Skinny rib you'll find useful, see it teamed with the matching pinafore dress on page 40

Materials: See Pinafore dress on page 40

BACK
With No. 11(2) needles and yellow, cast on 126(134,142) sts. and work in k.2, p.2 rib throughout.
1st row: K.2, p.2, to last 2 sts., k.2.
2nd row: P.2, k.2, to last 2 sts., p.2. Cont. thus until Back measures 16 ins. from beg.
Shape Armholes: Cast off 4(5,6) sts. at beg. of next 2 rows, then k.2 tog., at each end of next and every alt. row until 104 (108,112) sts. remain. Work without further shaping until Back measures 23¼ ins. from beg.
Shape Shoulder and Neck: Cast off 8 sts., rib 24(26,27) turn, k.2 tog., and work to end of row.
Next row: Cast off 7(8,8) sts., work to end. **Next row:** K.2 tog., at neck edge, work to end. Rep. these 2 rows. Cast off rem. sts. Place centre 40(40,42) sts. on a needle for neck. Rejoin wool to rem. sts. and complete to match other side.

FRONT
Work as for Back until Armhole measures 5½ ins. **Next row:** Rib 32(34,36) sts. turn. Now dec. 1 st. at neck edge on every row until 29(31,32) sts. remain. Cont. without further shaping until work matches back to shoulder, ending at side edge.
Shape Shoulder: Cast off 8 sts. at beg. of next row and 7(8,8) sts. on foll. 2 alt. rows. Work 1 row and cast off rem. sts. Return to sts. for other side and work to match.

SLEEVES
Cast on 50(54,54) sts. and work in rib as for Back for 20 rows. Now inc. 1 st. at each end of next and every foll. 8th row until there are 90(94,98) sts. on needle, taking increased sts. into rib pattern. Cont. without further shaping until sleeve measures 17½ ins.
Shape Top: Cast off 4(5,6) sts. at beg. of next 2 rows, then dec. 1 st. at each end of next and every foll. alt. row until 44(46,48) sts. rem. Now dec. 1 st. at each end of every row until 26 sts. rem. Cast off in rib.

ROLL COLLAR
Join left shoulder seam. Pick up and knit 136(140,140) sts. round neck. Work in k.2, p.2 rib for 6 ins. Cast off in rib.

TO MAKE UP
Do not Press. Join right shoulder seam and seam of roll collar. Set in sleeves. Join side and sleeve seams.

Chosen for Children

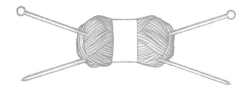

Special designs, each with a particular use in mind. Plain or
pretty, all will find a welcome with the mother of small folk as
a change from the usual knitting for children

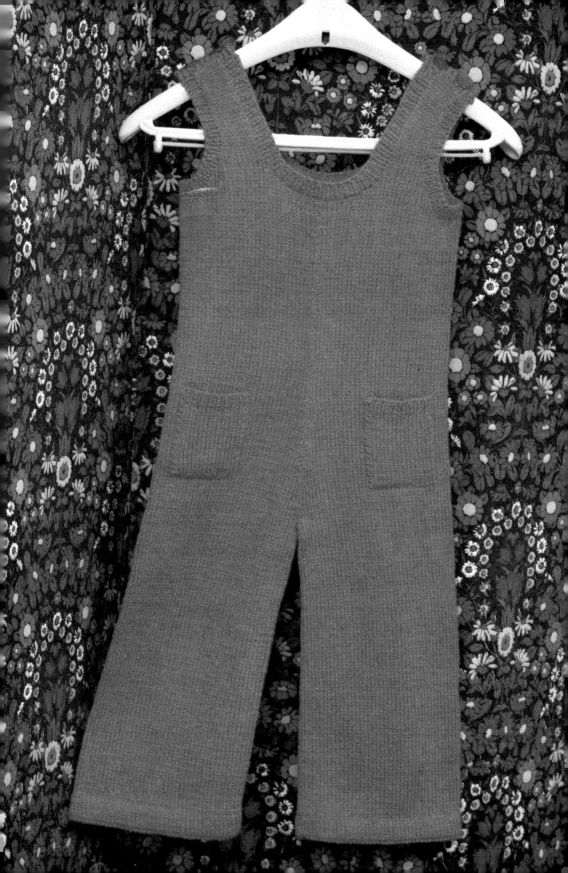

Child's Dungarees

for colour illustration, see page 63

Tough and cheerful for playtime, to wear with a variety of shirts and sweaters. Instructions are given for three sizes

Materials: 6(7,8) 50 gramme balls of Patons Trident Double Knitting; a pair each of Nos. 10(3) and 8(5) knitting needles; 4 buttons

Tension: 11 sts. and 15 rows to 2 ins. over st.st. on No. 8(5) needles.

Measurements: Chest: 22(24,26) ins. Leg seam: $12\frac{1}{2}(14,15\frac{1}{2})$ ins.; Centre Front seam: $11\frac{1}{2}(13\frac{1}{2},15\frac{1}{2})$ ins.

Abbreviations: See Page 10

Note: Instructions for the larger sizes are given in brackets. Where one figure only is given, this applies to all sizes.

RIGHT LEG

With No. 10(3) needles, cast on 80(86,92) sts. and work 7 rows st.st., beg. with a k. row. Knit next row to mark hemline. Change to No.8(5) needles and beg. with a k. row, cont. in st.st. until piece measures $12\frac{1}{2}(14,15\frac{1}{2})$ ins. from hemline, ending with a p. row. Place a marker at each end of last row and then shape as follows:

Cast off 2 sts. at beg. of next 2 rows, then dec. 1 st. at each end of 5th and every foll. 6th row until there are 64(70,76) sts. Cont. without further shaping until work measures $7\frac{1}{2}(8\frac{1}{2},9\frac{1}{2})$ ins. from markers, ending with a k. row.

Shape Back: 1st row: P.32(35, 38), turn.
2nd and every alt. row: K.
3rd row: P.24(27,29) turn.
5th row: P.16(19,20) turn.
7th row: P.8(11,11) turn. **9th row:** P. across all sts. Cont. without further shaping until work measures 11(13,15) ins. from markers, measuring at short edge of work, ending with a p. row.
Divide for Armhole: Next row: K.26 (29,32) turn and leave rem. sts. on a spare needle. **Next row:** P. Now dec. 1 st. at end of next row. Work 1 row straight.

Shape front neck and cont. to shape armhole: Next row: Cast off 7(8,9) sts., k. to last 2 sts. k.2 tog. Now dec. 1 st. at neck edge on every row and **at the same time** dec. 1 st. at armhole edge on every foll. alt. row until 11(13,15) sts. rem. Cont. to dec. at armhole edge, keeping neck edge straight, until 10 sts. rem. Work without further shaping until piece measures 16(18½,21) ins. from markers, measured at short edge of work, ending with a p. row. Leave these sts. on a spare needle. With right side facing, rejoin wool to sts. on first spare needle, cast off 12 and knit to end. Now work to match other side reversing shapings.

LEFT LEG
As for right leg, reversing all shapings.

POCKETS
With No. 8(5) needles, cast on 15(17,19) sts. and work as folls. K. 1 row.
Next row: K.1, p. to last st., k.1. Rep. last 2 rows for 22(24,26) rows. Change to No. 10(3) needles and work in k.1, p.1 rib for 4 rows. Cast off. Make another pocket to match.

TO MAKE UP
Press pieces lightly with a cool iron and a dry cloth. Sew pocket to each side of front. Join leg and front and back seams. With No. 10(3) needles and with right side facing, pick up and knit 68(74,80) sts. round each armhole. Work 4 rows k.1, p.1 rib. Cast off in rib.
Pick up and knit 66(76,86) sts. round Front neck border and work 5 rows k.1, p.1 rib. Cast off in rib. Work Back neck border to match.
Pick up and knit 4 sts. from rib at back shoulder, 10 sts. from spare needle, inc. 1 st. at centre and pick up and knit 4 sts. from other rib.
Next row: *P.1, k.1, to last st. p.1.
Next row: *K.1, p.1, to last st., k.1. Work 3 more rows in rib and cast off in rib. Work front shoulders to match, making buttonholes on 2nd and 3rd rows as folls:
2nd row: Rib 4, cast off 2, rib to last 6 sts., cast off 2, rib to end. **3rd row:** In rib, casting 2 sts. on over those cast off in previous row.
Fold hems of legs to wrong side and catch neatly into position. Press seams and add buttons to shoulders.

Toddler's Poncho and pants

Pretty lace stitch in three colours makes the pointed poncho. Make the pants to pick up the main colour, for the smartest babes in town

Materials: Poncho: 2 balls of Mahony's Blarney Berella Baby Quickerknit in White, 3 balls in pink and 2 balls of blue; **Pants:** 4 balls of blue for pants only; a pair each of Nos. 9(4), 10(3), and 11(2) knitting needles; a set of 4 double pointed needles Nos. 9(4) and 10(3); Elastic for waist.

Tension: 7 sts. to 1 inch over st.st., and 6 sts. to 1 inch over pattern on No. 9(4) needles.

Measurements: Poncho: Centre front seam: 15 ins.; **Pants:** Waist to crutch: $8\frac{1}{2}$ ins.; Inside leg seam: $10\frac{1}{4}$ ins., with ribbing turned up.

Abbreviations: See page 10

THE PONCHO

With No. 9(4) needles and white, cast on 191 sts. **1st row:** (wrong side) P.
2nd row: K.1, sl.1, k.1, p.s.s.o., p. to last 3 sts., k.2 tog., k.1. Rep. 1st and 2nd rows twice. Change to pink. **7th row:** P.
8th row: K.1, sl.1, k.2 tog., p.s.s.o., * y.fwd., k.3, y.fwd., sl.1, k.2 tog., p.s.s.o., rep. from * to last 7 sts., y.fwd., k.3, y.fwd., k.3 tog., k.1.
9th row and 11th row: P.
10th row: K.1, sl.1, k.1, p.s.s.o., * y.fwd., sl.1, k.2 tog., p.s.s.o., y.fwd., k.3, rep. from * to last 6 sts., y.fwd., sl.1, k.2 tog., p.s.s.o., y.fwd., k.2 tog., k.1.
12th row: K.1, sl.1, k.1, p.s.s.o., k.2 * y.fwd., sl.1, k.2 tog., p.s.s.o., y.fwd., k.3, rep. from * to last 8 sts., y.fwd., sl.1, k.2 tog., p.s.s.o., y.fwd., k.2, k.2 tog., k.1.
13th to 18th rows: As rows 7 to 12. Change to white. Rep. these 18 rows but use blue and pink in turn for 12 rows of lace patt., until 5 patts. and 6 rows of 6th patt. have been worked. Change to No.10 (3) needles and cont. to 18th row of 7th patt.
Next row: Still with pink, (p.2 tog., p.2) 15 times, p.2 tog., p.1, p.2 tog. Leave these sts. on a spare needle and make another piece to match. Now arrange all the sts. from both pieces on three No. 10 (3) needles, and with right side facing, and still with pink, knit 1 round and then work in k.2, p.2 rib for $1\frac{1}{2}$ ins. Change to set of No. 9(4) needles and work a further $2\frac{1}{2}$ ins. Cast off loosely in rib. Press lightly and join seams very neatly.

PANTS
Right Leg

With No. 11(2) needles and blue, cast on 81 sts. and work 14 rows in k.1, p.1 rib. Change to No. 9(4) needles and work 1 more row in rib. Purl 1 row then shape thus:
1st row: K.10, turn. **2nd and every**

Pram cover

wrong side row: Sl.1, p. to end.
3rd row: K.18, turn. **5th row:** K.26,
turn. **7th row:** K.34, turn. **9th row:**
K.42, turn. **10th row:** Sl.1, p.41. Cont.
in st.st. and inc. 1 st. at longer edge on
foll. 7th and every foll. 8th row until there
are 87 sts. Cont. without further shaping
until short edge measures 9 ins. ending
with a p. row.
Shape Leg: Cast off 3 sts. at beg. of next
2 rows, then dec. 1 st. at each end of next
5 rows. Now dec. 1 st. at each end of next
3 k. rows and then at each end of every
foll. 4th row 3 times. Cont. without
further shaping until leg measures $8\frac{1}{2}$
ins. ending with a p. row. Change to No.
11(2) needles. **Next row:** (K.2 tog., k.2)
14 times, k.2 tog., k.1. Now work $3\frac{1}{2}$ ins.
in k.2 p.2 rib. Cast off loosely in rib.
Work Left Leg to match reversing all
shapings.

TO MAKE UP

Press pieces lightly on wrong side. Join
front and back seams. Join inside leg seam
using flat seam for ribbing. Turn waist
ribbing in half to wrong side and catch
down. Insert elastic. Turn up ankle
ribbing. Press seams.

A very quick and easy gift to make for the
newcomer to your own family or for any
pram riding baby

Materials: Six 2 ozs. balls of Lister
Prema Bulky Knitting;
a pair of No. 5 knitting needles;
4 yds. of Blanket ribbon;
matching sewing silk.

Tension: 3 sts. to 1 inch.

Measurements: 18 by 24 ins. excluding
ribbon frill.

Abbreviations: See Page 10

TO MAKE

Cast on 57 sts. and knit 1 row. Now work
in pattern.
1st row: Slip 1, * k.1, k. into st. of row
below, rep. from * to last 2 sts. k.2.
2nd row: Slip 1, * k.1 into st. of row
below, k.1, rep. from * to end. These 2
rows form the pattern and are repeated.
Work in pattern until piece measures 24
ins. from beginning. Cast off loosely.

TO MAKE UP

Do not press. Open blanket ribbon out to
single thickness. Mark the centre of
length. Join into a circle. Mark a point
half way between the join and the marked
centre point on each side. Gather between
these points, gathering each single
thickness of ribbon. Pin evenly round
cover, folding the ribbon in half and
sewing each edge neatly to each side of
cover.

Sleeping bag for a baby

So many parents go camping and sailing, taking Junior too. Here's the ideal garment to keep a travelling child warm and cosy

Materials: Nine 50 gramme balls of Sirdar Candytwist; a pair each of Nos. 8(5) and 10(3) knitting needles; a 22 inch zip fastener; a length of shirring elastic.

Tension: $9\frac{1}{2}$ sts. to 2 ins. on No. 8(5) needles.

Measurements: Chest: 30 ins.; Length: at centre back 25 ins.; Sleeve: 8 ins.

Abbreviations: See Page 10

BACK AND FRONT

Working in one piece up to the armholes, with No. 8(5) needles, cast on 142 sts.
1st row: K.12, * (p.1, sl.2 purlwise with y.fwd.) 4 times, p.1, * k.92, rep. from * to * once, k.12.
2nd row: K.12, p.13, k.92, p.13, k.12.
3rd and 4th rows: As 1st and 2nd.
5th row: K. **6th row:** As 2nd. Rep. these 6 rows until work measures 18 ins.
Divide for Armholes: Next row: Patt. 33, cast off 4, k.68 including st. left on needle after casting off, cast off 4, patt. 33. Work on group of sts. for left front. K.12, p.13, k. to end.
1st row: K.2 tog., patt. to end.
2nd row: K.12, p.13, k. to end.
3rd row: Patt. to end. **4th row:** As 2nd. Rep. 1st and 2nd rows until 19 sts. remain, ending at neck edge.
Next row: Cast off 5, work to end. Still dec. at armhole edge as before and dec. 1 st. at neck edge. Work 1 row. Rep. last 2 rows until 5 sts. remain. Now dec. at armhole edge only until 2 sts. remain. Fasten off. Rejoin yarn to remaining sts.

for Back and with wrong side facing, k. to end.
Next row: K. 2 tog., k. to last 2 sts., k.2 tog. **Next row:** K. Repeat last 2 rows until 20 sts. remain. Cast off. Rejoin yarn to remaining sts. for Right Front and with wrong side facing, complete to match Left Front, reversing all shapings.

SLEEVES

With No. 10(3) needles, cast on 38 sts. and work in single rib for 4 rows. Change to No. 8(5) needles and cont. in g.st. Inc. 1 st. at each end of 7th and every foll. 8th row until there are 52 sts. on needle. Work without further shaping until sleeve measures $7\frac{1}{2}$ ins. from beg.
Shape Top: Cast off 2 sts. at beg. of next 2 rows. **Next row:** K.2 tog., k. to last 2 sts., k.2 tog. **Next 3 rows:** K. Rep. last 4 rows once more, then 1st and 2nd rows until 4 sts. remain. Cast off.

HOOD

With No. 10(3) cast on 84 sts. and work in single rib for 15 rows. Change to No. 8(5) needles and cont. in g.st. until work measures $6\frac{1}{2}$ ins.
Next row: K.1, k.2 tog., * k.2, k.2 tog., rep. from * to last st., k.1.
Next row: Cast off 23, k.17, cast off 23. Rejoin yarn to remaining sts. and cont. in g.st. Dec. 1 st. at each end of every 14th row until 13 sts. remain. Cont. without further shaping until work measures 5 ins. Cast off.

BOTTOM GUSSET

With No. 8(5) needles, cast on 40 sts. and knit 2 rows. Cont. in g.st. and cast on 4 sts. at beg. of next 2 rows. Then cast on 2 sts. at beg. of foll. 2 rows. Now inc. 1 st. at beg. of next 10 rows. Work 5 rows without further shaping. Now dec. 1 st. at beg. of

70

next 10 rows, cast off 2 sts. at beg. of foll.
2 rows and cast off 4 sts. at beg. of next 2
rows. Knit 2 rows. Cast off.

TO MAKE UP
Join sleeve and raglan seams. With wrong
side of sleeve facing, thread shirring
elastic through first 4 rows at lower edge of
sleeve. Set in zip fastener. Set Hood to
neck and set gusset into lower edge.

Baby's carrying cape

Smarter than a shawl and ideal for the Babe in arms. Simple stocking stitch in pink is striped with pattern in white

Materials: 5 balls of Mahony's Blarney Berella Baby Quickerknit in main colour and 2 balls in contrast;
a pair each of Nos. 8(5) and 10(3) knitting needles;
3 buttons;
1 yd. of 1 inch facing ribbon;
1 yd. of narrow ribbon for neck tie.

Tension: 6¼ sts. and 8 rows to 1 inch on No. 8(5) needles.

Measurements: Length from Neck: 21½ ins. All round lower edge: 42 ins.

Abbreviations: See page 10

TO MAKE

With No. 8(5) needles and main colour, cast on 278 sts. and p. 5 rows. Change to No. 10(3) needles and contrast.
1st row: (wrong side) P.
2nd row: K.1, then k.2 tog., to last st., k.1.
3rd row: K.1, * p.u.k. winding yarn twice round needle, k.1 winding yarn twice round needle, rep. from * to last st. k.1. **Note** Do not work into thread before last st.
4th row: K. dropping extra loops. Change to No. 8(5) needles and main colour. **5th row:** P.
6th row: P.4, k. to last 4 sts., p.4.
7th to 18th rows: Rep. 5th and 6th rows 6 times. Change to No. 10(3) needles and contrast. These 18 rows form the pattern. Rep. them once more then rows 1 to 17 again.
Next row: P.4, k.2, (k.2 tog., k.10, k.2 tog.) 19 times, k.2, p.4. Work 35 rows of pattern on these sts.
Next row: P.4, k.2, (k.2 tog., k.8, k.2

tog.) 19 times, k.2, p.4. Work 35 rows of patt. on these sts.
Next row: P.4, k.2, (k.2 tog., k.6, k.2 tog.) 19 times, k.2, p.4. Work 17 rows of patt. on these sts.
Next row: P.4, k.1, (k.2 tog., k.4, k.2 tog.) 19 times, k.1, p.4. Work 5 rows of patt. on these sts. Cont. in k.2, p.2 rib keeping garter st. borders. Make buttonhole in 4th row thus: Work to last 4 sts., y.r.n., p.2 tog., p.2. Work 8 rows in rib with garter st. borders.
Next row: P.4, (k.2, p.2 tog.) to last 6 sts., k.2, p.4.
Next row: P.4, (p.2, k.1) to last 6 sts., p.2, y.r.n., p.2 tog., p.2. Work 6 more rows with centre sts. in k.2, p.1 rib.
Next row: P.4, (k.2 tog., p.1) to last 6 sts., k.2 tog., p.4. Change to No. 10(3) needles and work 2 rows with centre sts. in p.1, k.1 rib. Make a buttonhole on next row then work 6 more rows.
Next row: P.4, (y.o.n., k.2 tog., k.1, y. fwd., k.2 tog., p.1) 10 times, p.3. Work 3 more rows with centre sts. in rib as before but inc. 1 st. in centre of last row
Next row: Cast off 8, k.7, (including st. on needle), (inc. into next st., k.2) 6 times, inc. into next st., turn. Change to No. 8(5) needles and work on these sts. for one side of hood. **1st row:** P. **2nd row:** P.4, k. to end. Rep. these 2 rows once. * Now beg. with 1st row, work in patt. as for main part but with border at front edge only. Inc. 1 st. at other edge on 2nd and 11th rows of each st.st. band until 36 rows have been worked from *. Work 7 rows without further shaping, then dec. 1 st. at shaped edge on alt. rows 3 times, then on every row 4 times. Cast off rem. sts. Rejoin yarn to rem. sts. at centre.
1st row: (With right side facing) Inc. into 1st stitch, (k.2, inc. into next st.) 6 times, k.7, cast off 8 sts. Break yarn and rejoin at needle point. Complete to match first side of hood, reversing border and shaping.

TO MAKE UP

Press lightly with a dry cloth and a warm iron. Face front edges neatly with ribbon as far as base of yoke. Add buttons. Join back and top seam of hood. Thread ribbon through holes at neck and tie in a bow.

It's in the bag

One needs a bag for so many things. All these are easy and one can be made in less than an evening. Most of them would take only two evenings to complete. From a washable shopping bag to one for the evening, take one to the beach or carry your playing cards in it, make one to match a summer outfit, all of them have that certain flair to make them different

White fringed bag

Big needles and thick yarn for a bag you can easily make in one evening. Line it with a bright contrasting colour or keep it in white to go with anything

Materials: Two 50 yard hanks of Twilley's 747 Orlon Sayelle; a pair of $\frac{1}{2}$ inch Whizz-pins; crochet hook for fringing.

Measurements: Width: 11 ins. Depth 10 ins.

Abbreviations: See page 10

Note: This bag takes about 2 hours to make.

TO MAKE
Main Part: Cast on 20 sts. and work in garter stitch for 70 rows. Cast off.
Strap: Cast on 3 sts. and work 82 rows in garter stitch. Cast off.

TO MAKE UP
Leave 14 rows at cast on edge of main part for flap. Fold remaining rows in half and join sides. Turn to right side and sew ends of strap inside at sides below flap. Cut remaining yarn into 17 in. lengths. Using 2 strands at a time, knot for fringing through every stitch along lower edge. Using one strand at a time, fringe through every stitch along edge of flap.

Shopping bag

That old string bag, you remember, you used it to cart the vegetables home and it wore out. Make another, it's easy and washable

Materials: 2 balls of Twilley's Stalite cotton No. 3;
a pair each of Nos. 12(1) and 9(4) knitting needles.

Tension: $6\frac{1}{2}$ sts. and $8\frac{1}{2}$ rows to 1 inch on No. 9(4) needles.

Measurements: Width: 18 ins. all round;

Length: 13 ins.

Abbreviations: See page 10

TO MAKE

With No. 12(1) needles, cast on 9 sts. and knit 1 row.
1st inc. row: * (K.1, p.u.k.) twice, k.1, rep. from * twice more.
Next row: Knit. (15 sts.)
2nd inc. row: * (K.1, p.u.k.) 4 times, k.1, rep. from * twice more.
Next row: Knit. (27 sts.)
3rd inc. row: * (K.1, p.u.k.) 8 times, k.1, rep. from * twice more.
Next row: Knit. (51 sts.)
4th inc. row: * (K.1, p.u.k.) 16 times, k.1, rep. from * twice more.
Next row: Knit (99 sts.) Change to No. 9 (4) needles and pattern.
1st row: K.1, * y.r.n., k.2 tog., rep. from * to end. **2nd row:** Knit. Rep. these 2 rows for a further 12 ins. Change to g. st. Knit 6 rows. Cast off. Press lightly. Join seam. Make a twisted cord and thread through first row of holes below garter stitch border.

Yellow tote bag

You see them around all over the place, so you really should have one. This is another two row pattern and one for which you can change the colour on every two rows, so odd balls will make a very cheerful bag, and cost you nothing

Materials: Two 50 gramme balls of Patons Double Knitting Wool in Yellow, gold and orange;
a pair of No. 9(4) knitting needles;
4 brass rings;
lining material to match.

Tension: 6 sts. and 8 rows to 1 inch over pattern.

Measurements: Width: 12 ins., Depth: 15 ins.

Abbreviations: See page 10

TO MAKE
With Yellow, cast on 72 sts. and work 2 ins. in garter stitch. Now begin pattern.
1st row: (Wrong side) Purl.
2nd row: K.2, * w.r.n., k.3, pass first of 3 knit sts. over 2nd and 3rd sts., rep. from * to last st. k.1. Change to gold. **3rd row:** Purl.
4th row: K.1, * k.3, pass first of 3 knit sts. over 2nd and 3rd sts., w.r.n., rep. from * to last 2 sts., k.2. Change to orange and repeat pattern, using each colour in turn for 2 rows. Continue until piece measures 30 ins., ending with yellow. Now work a further 2 ins. in garter stitch and cast off.

TO MAKE UP
Press piece on wrong side lightly. Cut lining material to match, less the 2 ins. of garter stitch at each end. Fold lining in half and join both long sides, leaving one narrow end open. Join seams of knitted piece in same way. Insert lining and turn the 2 ins. of garter stitch inside over the edge of lining and sew neatly into place. Make a thick twisted cord 72 inches long. Sew two brass rings to each side of top about 2 ins. from each end. Thread cord through rings and tie in a knot to form double handle.

Striped summer handbag

Two straight pieces and easy knitting. You could make more than one and have them to match your summer wardrobe

Materials: 2 balls each of Twilley's Lysbet in Mauve and Purple;
a pair of No. 10(3) knitting needles;
a pair of circular handles 5 ins. diameter;
lining material to match.

Tension: 7 sts. and 9 rows to 1 inch.

Measurements: Width: 13 ins., **Depth:** 10 ins.

Abbreviations: See page 10

TO MAKE

With Mauve, cast on 80 sts. and work $1\frac{1}{4}$ ins. Change to purple and work $1\frac{1}{4}$ ins. Cont. in this way until 4 purple and 5 mauve stripes have been worked. Cast off. Make another piece to match. Press lightly with a cool iron over a dry cloth. Cut lining to match. Join seams of lining and knitted pieces, leaving one wide edge open for top. Insert lining. Begin $1\frac{1}{2}$ ins. from one side and insert a handle, sewing knitted piece over handle to lining. Insert second handle in same way. Neatly join lining and knitted edges at sides. Trim lower corners with a tassel.

Orange and white beach bag

In thick cotton and a simple two row pattern which makes the points at top and bottom. You will find many uses for this bag

Materials: 3 balls of Twilley's Knitcot in White and 2 balls Tango; a pair of No. 9(4) knitting needles; a pair of handles approx. 10 ins. wide; 3/4 yd. of 1 in. wide binding; towel lining.

Tension: 6¼ sts. and 6 rows to 1 inch over pattern.

Measurements: Width: 13 ins.; Length: 14 ins.

Abbreviations: See page 10

TO MAKE

With White, cast on 87 sts. and work in patt. as follows.
1st row: (Right side) K.1, sl.1, k.1, p.s.s.o., *
k.9, sl.2, k.1, p.2 s.s.o., rep. from * to last 12 sts., k.9, k.2 tog., k.1.
2nd row: K.1, * p.1, k.4, (k.1, y.o.n., k.1) all into next st., k.4, rep. from * to last 2 sts., p.1, k.1. Change to Tango. **3rd and 4th rows:** As 1st and 2nd rows.
Repeat these 4 rows, changing colour on right side rows, working 2 rows in each colour in turn until piece measures 14 ins., ending with white and 2nd row. Cast off loosely. Make another piece.

TO MAKE UP

Press pieces lightly. Cut two pieces of lining to match. Join three sides leaving one narrow end open. Join seams of knitted pieces in same way, leaving cast off edges open for top. Insert lining. Join one edge of binding to top of bag at lower edge of points. Insert frame of handle under binding and sew other edge of binding to lining. Complete other side, inserting second handle. Trim points at bottom of bag with alternate tassels of white and tango.

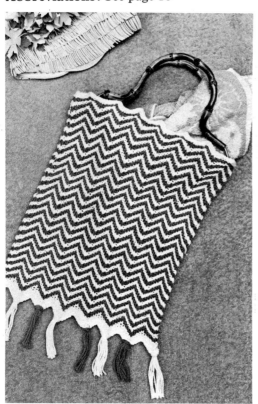

Evening bag

Knit a bit of glamour to carry those bits
and pieces you must have with you, even
on the best occasions. It is very easy,
fringes make the magic

Materials: 3 ozs. Twilley's Goldfingering
in Silver and 1 oz. each in Copper and
Pewter;
a pair of No. 11(2) knitting needles;
a medium sized crochet hook for fringing.

Tension: 7 sts. and 14 rows to 1 inch.

Measurements: Width: 7 ins. Depth: 9
ins.

Abbreviations: See Page 10

TO MAKE
With No.11(2) needles and Silver, cast on
50 sts. and work 18 ins. garter stitch. Cast
off.
Strap: Cast on 4 sts. in silver and work
34 ins. g. st. Cast off.

TO MAKE UP
Do not press. Fold main part in half and
join sides, Sew ends of strap to each side.
To Fringe: With silver, cut 6 strands
each 16 ins. long, fold in half and with
crochet hook, knot through every 3rd
stitch round top of bag. With Copper,
fringe in same way into every 3rd stitch
round centre. With Pewter, fringe round
lower edge into every 3rd stitch. Trim
fringes neatly.

Toy cupboard

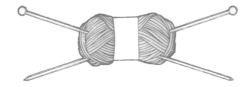

Soft toys quickly become constant companions for a small child. In order to make sure they will last as long as the love of their owner, do make certain that the pieces are all very well and firmly stuffed. Stitch pieces together firmly and take a little time to make them as nearly indestructible as possible. Never use buttons or eyes with pins or anything a small child can detach and swallow. A toy will then be a joy and never a sorrow to anyone.

There is a small bonus for Dad, in a set of covers for his golf clubs, so don't leave him out.

Since a poncho is still so popular, every smart doll should have one too. This one is very simple to make

Pink elephant

for colour illustration, see page 7

A fat and cuddly elephant for a change.
She might have come straight from
Toyland Zoo

Materials: Ten 25 gramme balls of
Machine Washable Emu Double Knitting
Wool;
scraps of felt for ears, eyes, feet and
flower;
washable stuffing;
a pair of No. 10(3) knitting needles.

Tension: 7 sts. and 8 rows to 1 inch.

Measurements: Height: 9 ins.; Length:
17 ins.

Abbreviations: See page 10

TO MAKE

1st Side:
Cast on 8 sts. and work 2 rows st.st.
Cast on 5 sts. at beg. of next 4 rows.
7th row: Cast on 34 sts., k. to end.
8th row: Purl. **9th row:** Cast on 3 sts.
at beg. of row, k. to last st., k. twice into
last st. **10th row:** P. twice into first and
last sts. **11th row:** As 9th. **12th row:** P.
to last st., p. twice into last st. Repeat last
4 rows once more.
17th row: K. twice into 1st and last st.
18th row: As 12th. Repeat last 2 rows
twice more. **23rd row:** K. twice into
1st st., k. to end. **24th row:** As 12th.
25th row: As 17th. **26th row:** Purl.
27th row: As 23rd. **28th row:** Purl.
Repeat last 4 rows once more.
33rd row: As 17th. **34th row:** P. twice
into 1st st., p. to end. **35th row:** K. to
last st., k. twice into last st.
36th row: P. Repeat last 4 rows once
more. (109) sts.
41st row: As 35th. **42nd row:** As 34th.
43rd row: As 35th. **44th row:** Purl.
45th row: K.98, turn, leaving 14 sts.
on spare needle. Work 3 rows st.st.
49th row: K.80, cast off 3 sts., k.8 turn.
Leave last 7 sts. on needle. **50th row:**

Working on the 8 sts. p.2 tog. at each end
of row. **51st row:** K.2 tog. at each end of
row. Cast off last 4 sts. Rejoin wool at
inner edge of the 7 sts. Cast off 2, k.5.
Next row: P.3, p.2 tog.
Next row: K.2 tog., k.2. **Next row:** P.1,
p.2 tog. Cast off last 2 sts.
Rejoin wool at inner edge of the 80 sts.
Next row: P.2 tog., p. to end.
Next row: K. Repeat last 2 rows 3 times
more. (76) sts. Work 13 rows st.st. ★
Next row: K.50, k.2 tog., k. to end. Leave
50 sts. on a spare needle.
Next row: P. to last 2 sts., p.2 tog.
Next row: K.2 tog., k. to end. Repeat
last 2 rows once more.
Next row: P. to last 2 sts., p.2 tog.
Work 16 rows st.st. Cast off last 20 sts.
With wrong side facing, rejoin wool to
inner edge of 50 sts. on spare needle. Cast
off 25 sts., p. to end. **Next row:** K. to
last 2 sts., k.2 tog.
Next row: P.2 tog., p. to end. Repeat
last 2 rows once more. K. to last 2 sts. k.2
tog. Work 16 rows st.st. Cast off last 20
sts. ★
Rejoin wool to inner edge of 14 sts. with
right side facing.
1st row: Cast off 5, k. to last st., k. twice
into last st.
2nd row: Cast on 2 sts., p. to last 2 sts.,
p.2 tog. **3rd row:** Cast off 2 sts., k. to last
st., k. twice into last st. **4th row:** As 2nd.
Repeat last 2 rows 3 times more. Now dec.
1 st. at each end of next 4 rows.
Next row: K.2 tog., k.1. Cast off. Make
another side to match reversing shaping.
Underside:
Cast on 36 sts. Work 2 rows st.st. Cast on
10 sts. at beg. of next 4 rows. Work 8 rows
st.st. Cont. as for first side from ★ to ★
Make another piece to match.
Rear section: Cast on 8 sts. Work 16
rows st.st. **17th row:** K. twice into 1st
stitch, k. to end.
18th row: P. to last st., p. twice into last
st. Repeat last 2 rows twice more. (14 sts.)
Cast on 14 sts. at beg. of next row. Do not

Little lamb

for colour illustration, see page 89

knit across row. Break wool. Now cast on 8 sts. on the same needle holding the 28 sts. Work 16 rows st.st. on 8 sts. **17th row:** K. to last st., k. twice into last st. **18th row:** P. twice into 1st stitch, p. to end. Repeat last 2 rows twice more. (14 sts.) All 42 sts. should now be on the same needle. Two legs with 14 cast on sts. in centre. Work 8 rows st.st. * **Next row:** K.2 tog., at each end of row. **Next row:** P. Repeat last 2 rows 3 times more. Take 2 tog. at each end of next 3 rows. **Next row:** P. Repeat last 4 rows 3 times more. Take 2 tog. at each end of next 4 rows. Cast off last 2 sts.

Chest:
Work as for rear section from beg. to * Take 2 tog. at each end of next 3 rows. **Next row:** P. Repeat last 4 rows 3 times more. Take 2 tog. at each end of next row. Work 2 rows st.st. Repeat last 3 rows. Take 2 tog. at each end of next row. Next row: P. Work 20 rows st.st. Cast off last 12 sts.

Trunk Under-section:
Cast on 12 sts. and work 4 rows st.st. **Next row:** K.2 tog., at each end. Work 5 rows st.st. Repeat last 6 rows twice more. Inc. 1 st. into first st. of next 4 rows. Work 1 row. Cast off 10 sts.

TO MAKE UP

Press all pieces carefully. Join side sections together starting at trunk and ending approx. 5 ins. beyond cast on edge. Set rear section into back neatly. Set in trunk under-section and sew in chest section. Join 2 under sections, leaving 4 ins. open on straight edge for stuffing. Sew to sides of elephant, matching legs, etc.
Cut two ears in felt and sew to head. Make eyes from felt scraps and add to face. Cut 4 circles of felt and sew to bottom of feet and a small circle to end of trunk. Stuff firmly and close opening. Make a tail in plaited wool and attach to back. Embroider toes on feet. Add a flower to mouth.

A very attractive toy to find a place in any child's heart

Materials: 10 ozs. Emu Machine Washable Double Knitting Wool in white; 2 ozs. in Black; washable stuffing; strip of ribbon or felt for collar; 3 bells; scraps of felt or embroidery wool for features; a pair of No. 10(3) knitting needles.

Tension: 6 sts. and 8 rows to 1 inch over st.st.

Measurements: Height: approx. 13 ins.

Abbreviations: See Page 10

TO MAKE
Side of Body:
Beg. with front leg, cast on 14 sts. in Black wool. Work 8 rows st.st.
9th row: Change to white and knit.
10th row: K.1, k.1 winding wool twice round needle and first finger, then round needle only, draw loops through, slipping original st. off left hand needle. Holding loops at back of work, slip loops back on to left hand needle and knit them together through back of loops. Repeat these loop sts. to last st., k.1. Repeat last 2 rows until 42nd row has been worked. Leave sts. on a spare needle. For Back leg work as for front leg until 30th row has been completed.
31st row: Inc. 1 st. at end of row. Work 3 rows straight.
35th row: K.2 tog. at beg. of row and inc. 1 st. at end. **36 and 38th row:** Loop Row.
37th and 39th rows: As 35th row. Work 3 rows straight.
43rd row: K.2 tog., k. to end of row, turn and cast on 10 sts., then knit across the 14 sts. on spare needle. Cont. to work 44th and every even row in loop stitch.

45th row: Inc. 1 st. into first st. work to end.
47th row: Inc. into last st.
49th row: As 45th row. (41 sts.)
50th row: Loop st. Repeat 9th and 10th rows 3 times.
57th row: K.2 tog., work to end. Dec. in same way on odd rows 3 times more.
65th row: K.2 tog. at each end. **67th row:** As 57th. Dec. at each end of next odd row.
71st row: Cast off 18 sts. at beg. of row. (14 sts.)
73rd row: As 57th. **75th row:** As 57th. Cast off.
Making another piece to match but reversing shapings and work the back leg first. 43rd row will read: Knit to end of row, turn and cast on 10 sts., knit across back leg sts. to last 2 sts., k.2 tog.

Underbody (first side)
Work as for first body side but in st.st. only. Work to completion of 44th row (38 sts.)
45th row: Cast off 6 sts., work to end.
47th row: Cast off 6 sts. work to end, increase at end of row. **49th row:** As 45th.
51st row: As 45th. **53rd row:** Cast off 7 sts. at beg. of row, work to end.
55th row: Cast off.
Work 2nd side to match reversing shapings, as for second body side but in st.st. to end of 42nd row.
43rd row: Knit to end of row, turn and cast on 10 sts., knit across back leg sts., to last 2 sts., k.2 tog.
44th row: Cast off 6 sts. at beg. of row.
46th row: As 44th.
48th row: Cast off 6 sts., work to last st., inc. into last st.
50th row: As 44th. **52nd row:** Cast off 7 sts. at beg. of row. Cast off.

TO MAKE UP BODY

Join two under body pieces along upper cast off edge. Place the joined pieces between sides of body, matching the legs and seam into place. Seam body sides together above front and back legs along back but leave cast off edge open. Stuff evenly and firmly.
Tail:
With White wool, cast on 8 sts.
1st row: Knit. **2nd row:** Loop st. Cont. in this way and inc. 1 st. at each end of next row, then work straight until 26 rows have been worked. Cast off and make another piece to match, but in st.st. for under side of tail.
Join pieces together, leaving cast off edge open. Turn to right side, join open end and stitch firmly to back.
Side of Head:
With White wool, cast on 18 sts. Work 6 rows st.st.
7th row: Inc. into 1st stitch, knit to end, turn and cast on 3 sts.
8th row: P. to last 8 sts., loop st. 7, k.1.
9th row: Inc. 1 st. at each end of row.
10th row: Inc. into first st., p. to last 8 sts., loop st. 7, k.1.
11th row: As 9th. **12th row:** As 10th.
13th row: K. **14th row:** P. to last 8 sts., loop st. 7, k.1. **15th row:** K.
16th row: P. to last 7 sts., loop st. 6, k.1. **17th row:** K.
18th row: P. to last 6 sts., loop st. 5, k.1. **19th row:** K.
20th row: P. to last 5 sts., loop st. 4, k.1.
21st row: K. **22nd row:** As 20th.
23rd row: Inc. 1 st. at beg. of row. (29 sts.)
24th row: As 20th. **25th row:** K.2 tog., at end of row. (Tie in a coloured marker to first st.)
26th row: P.2 tog., p. to last 5 sts., loop st. 4, k.1. **27th row:** K.2 tog., at end of row.
28th row: P.2 tog., work to last 5 sts., loop st. 4, k.1. **29th row:** K. **30th row:** P. to last 5 sts., loop st. 4, k.1. **31st row:** K. Repeat last 2 rows three times.
38th row: As 30th row. **39th row:** K.2 tog. at each end of row. **40th row:** As

Harry hedgehog

30th. **41st row:** As 39th. **42nd row:** As 30th. **43rd row:** K.2 tog., across row to last st., k.1. **44th row:** As 30th. Cast off. Make another piece to match, reversing shapings and loops will be at beg. of rows.
Head Gusset.
With White wool, cast on 4 sts. and work 6 rows in st.st. **7th row:** Inc. 1 st. at each end of knit row.
8th row: P. **9th row:** As 7th. **10th row:** P. **11th row:** As 7th. **12th row:** P.
13th row: As 7th. (12 sts.) **14th row:** K.1, loop st. to last st., k.1. **15th row:** K. Repeat these 2 rows to end of 50th row.
51st row: K.2 tog., at each end of next and alt. rows until 2 sts. remain. Cast off.

TO MAKE UP HEAD

Place the head gusset between sides of head, placing cast on edge of gusset level with the coloured marker on head sides. Seam gusset into place. Then seam head sides together from side to side, above and below gusset leaving cast on edge of head sides open. Stuff firmly and carefully. Stitch head very firmly to body.
Muzzle:
With Black wool, cast on 12 sts. and work in st.st.
1st row: P. **2nd row:** Inc. 1 st. at each end of next row. Repeat these 2 rows until there are 20 sts. on needle. Cont. in st.st. until 13 rows have been completed from beg.
14th row: K.2 tog., at each end of this and every foll. alt. row until 12 sts. remain. Cast off. Run a thread of wool round edge of muzzle, pull up slightly and stuff slightly. Sew to head at nose, over base of gusset. Embroider features or cut out in scraps of felt and sew to face.
Ears:
With black wool, make 4 pieces as for tail. 2 in st.st. for inner ear and 2 in loop st. Join the pieces together and attach to head. Join three bells to collar and fit round neck.

Harry's happy in the garden and he could be made in an evening, ready to greet a new owner in the morning

Materials One 50 gramme ball of Patons Double Knitting Wool; a pair of No. 9(4) knitting needles · scraps of Red and White wool for features; stuffing.

Measurements: Length: 7 ins.

Abbreviations: See page 10

BODY AND HEAD

Cast on 25 sts.
1st row: (Right side) Purl.
2nd row: *K.1, M.L., rep. from * to last st. k.1. **3rd row:** Purl. **4th row:** M.L., * K.1, M.L., rep. from * to end. These 4 rows form the pattern. Continue until piece measures $4\frac{1}{2}$ ins. Change to garter stitch and work as follows:
1st row: K.2 tog., k. to last 2 sts., k.2 tog.
2nd row: Knit. Rep. last 2 rows until 9 sts. remain, ending with 2nd row. Cast off.

UNDER BODY

Cast on 15 sts. and work 6 rows in loop pattern then work 35 rows in garter stitch.
Next row: K.2 tog., k. to last 2 sts., k.2 tog., **Next row:** Knit. Rep. these 2 rows until 7 sts. remain, ending with 2nd row. Cast off.

FEET

Cast on 12 sts. and work 6 rows garter stitch. **Next row:** K.2 tog. to end. Break wool, thread through remaining sts., draw up and secure. Fold piece in half and join seam. Make three more to match.

TO MAKE

Join body and under body together, leaving an opening for stuffing. Stuff firmly and shape head carefully. Sew up opening. Sew feet to under body. Embroider white eyes and red mouth.

Golf club covers

Something for Dad and not difficult to make. You could make them all in the same colour, lengthen the rib and work one stripe of contrast in the ribbing to mark No. 1 cover. Mark each cover with the right number of stripes

Materials: 2 ozs. each in Lister Lavenda Double Six Wool in Blue, red, emerald and gold;
a pair each of Nos. 7(6), 8(5) and 9(4) knitting needles;
a medium sized crochet hook.

Tension: $5\frac{1}{2}$ sts. and 7 rows to 1 inch.

Measurements: To fit Nos. 4,3,2 and 1 clubs approx. $8\frac{3}{4}$ ins in length.

Abbreviations: See Page 10

TO MAKE

No. 4 Cover

With Blue and No. 8(5) needles, cast on 50 sts.
** **1st row:** K.2, * p.2, k.2, rep. from * to end. **2nd row:** K.2, * p.2, k.2, rep. from * to end. Rep. these 2 rows 5 times more, change to No. 9(4) needles and cont. until piece measures 3 ins. from beg., ending with 2nd row. Make holes for cord.
Next row: * K.2, w.r.n., p.2 tog., rep. from * to last 2 sts., k.2. Change to No. 8 (5) needles and beg. with 2nd row, work 3 rows in rib and inc. 1 st. at end of last row. Change to No. 7(6) needles and rice stitch.
1st row: * K.1 t.b.l., p.1, rep. from * to last st., k.1 t.b.l.
2nd row: K. These 2 rows form rice st. Cont. until piece measures $7\frac{1}{2}$ ins. from beg., ending with 2nd row. **
Shape Top: 1st row: K.1, (RS.8, k.2 tog.) 5 times. **2nd row:** (k.2 tog. t.b.l., k.7) 5 times, k.1. **3rd row:** K.1, (RS.6, k.2 tog.) 5 times. **4th row:** (K.2 tog. t.b.l.,

k.5) 5 times, k.1. Cont. to shape thus until **9th row:** K.1, (k.2 tog.) 5 times has been completed. Cut wool and secure rem. sts.
No. 3 cover: Work as for No. 4 but casting on 54 sts. and red wool, working from ** to **. Shape top by beg. **1st row:** (RS. 9, k.2 tog.) 5 times. Cont. to shape as for No. 4 cover.
No. 2 cover: Work as for No. 4 casting on 58 sts. in emerald. Shape top thus:
1st row: (RS.8, k.2 tog.) 5 times, RS.9.
2nd row: (K. 2 tog. t.b.l., k.7) 6 times.
3rd row: (RS.6, k.2 tog.) 6 times.
4th row: (K.2 tog. t.b.l., k.5) 6 times. Finish in same way.
No. 1 cover: As for No. 4 but cast on 62 sts. in gold. **Shape top:** (RS.8, k.2 tog.) 6 times, RS.3. **2nd row:** K.3, (k.2 tog. t.b.l., k.7) 6 times.
3rd row: (RS.6, k.2 tog.) 6 times, RS.3.
4th row: K.3, (k.2 tog. t.b.l., k.5) 6 times. Cont. to 8th and 9th row and work **8th row:** (K.2 tog. t.b.l., k.1) 7 times.
9th row: (K.2 tog.) 7 times. Finish as before.
Join seams and press. Make a crochet cord and thread through holes in each cover.

Mick monkey

Cute little chap from the jungle to make mostly in garter stitch, with very little shaping

Materials: Three 50 gramme balls of Patons Limelight Double Crepe in Brown and 1 in fawn;
a pair of No. 8(5) knitting needles;
stuffing;
a scrap of white wool for features.

Tension: 11 sts. to 2 ins. over st.st.

Measurements: Height: 21 ins. approx.

Abbreviations: See Page 10

BODY
With Brown cast on 10 sts. and work in garter stitch. Knit 1 row. Now cast on 4 sts. at beg. of next 4 rows. (26 sts.) Cont. on these sts. until piece measures 6 ins. from beg. Cast off 8 sts. at beg. of next 2 rows. Work 8 rows on remaining sts. Cast off. Make another piece to match.

LEGS
With Brown, cast on 24 sts. and work 100 rows in garter stitch, placing a marker at each end of 33rd and 67th rows. Cast off. Make another leg.

ARMS
With Brown, cast on 20 sts. and work 80 rows in garter stitch. Place a marker at each end of 31st and 51st rows. Cast off. Make another Arm.

HANDS
With Brown cast on 4 sts. and work in st.st., beg. with a k. row. Inc. 1 st. at each end of 2nd and every alt. row until there are 10 sts. Work 4 rows straight. Now dec. 1 st. at each end of every 3rd row until 6 sts. remain. Cast off. Make another piece in Brown and 2 pieces to match in fawn.

FEET
With Brown cast on 8 sts. and work in st.st., beg. with a k. row. Inc. 1 st. at each end of 2nd and every alt. row until there are 12 sts. Work 6 rows straight. Now dec. 1 st. at each end of every 3rd row until 8 sts. remain. Cast off. Make another piece in Brown and 2 pieces in fawn.

EARS
With Fawn, cast on 11 sts. and work in st.st., beg. with a k. row. Work 3 rows. Now dec. 1 st. at each end of next row. Rep. these 4 rows once more, Cast off. Make 3 more pieces.

BACK OF HEAD
With Brown, cast on 10 sts. and work 8 rows in garter stitch.
Next row: Inc. into 1st st., k. to end.
Next row: K. Rep. these 2 rows 3 times more. (14 sts.)
Next row: Inc. into 1st stitch, k. to last 2 sts., k.2 tog., **Next row:** K. Rep. these 2 rows 4 times in all.
Next row: K. Rep. these 2 rows until there are 20 sts. Work 10 rows straight. Cast off 4 sts. at beg. (shaped edge) of next and foll. 3 alt. rows. Work 1 row straight. Cast off. Make another piece.

FRONT OF HEAD
With Fawn, cast on 24 sts. and work 8 rows in st.st., beg. with a k. row.
Next row: K.4, sl.1, k.1, p.s.s.o., k. to last 6 sts., k.2 tog., k. to end. **Next row:** Purl. Rep. these 2 rows 5 times in all. (14 sts.) Cast off. Make another piece to match.

Doll's poncho

TAIL

With Brown, cast on 12 sts. and work 3 ins. in garter stitch. Place a marker at each end of next row and work a further 3 ins. Place another marker and work another 3 ins, Cast off.

TO MAKE UP

With Brown, gather slightly between markers on legs, arms and tail. Fold each piece in half lengthwise and join seam firmly, leaving ends open. Turn to right side and stuff firmly. Close ends. Take care to retain curves while stuffing these parts. For hands and feet, take a brown and fawn piece and place together. Join firmly, leaving cast-on edge open. Turn to right side and stuff firmly. Close opening. For Ears, finish as for hands and feet, using 2 pieces of fawn together. With curves of legs and arms facing outwards, join hands and feet with fawn sides facing outwards. Embroider fingers and toes in Brown.

Join two body pieces together firmly, and stuff but leave neck open. Join arms, legs and tail to body. Join shaped edges of two pieces for back of head and join two pieces for face in same way, leaving cast-on edge open. Place a little stuffing in back and front of head and sew into position, matching centre seam. Continue to stuff head through neck, placing extra stuffing round mouth. Join ears to head, gathering cast-on edges slightly. When head and body are both firmly stuffed, join head to body. Embroider eyes, nose and mouth in Brown and White.

A fashionable cover-up for that doll who never has a thing to wear. Made in the time it takes you to knit up two ounces of double knitting wool

Materials: 2 ozs. Sirdar Double Knitting Wool in Main colour; 1 oz. contrast; a pair of No. 8(5) knitting needles; a medium sized crochet hook.

Tension: $5\frac{1}{2}$ sts. and $7\frac{1}{2}$ rows to 1 inch.

Measurements: To fit a 16 inch doll.

Abbreviations: See Page 10

TO MAKE

With main colour, cast on 60 sts. Knit 1 row and purl 1 row. Cont. in st.st. and dec. 1 st. at each end of every k. row until 22 sts. remain. Leave these sts. on a spare needle and make another piece to match. Now, with right side facing and contrast colour, knit across both sets of sts. Work 12 rows k.1, p.1 rib. Cast off. Press and join seams. With the crochet hook, and contrast wool, work 2 rows double crochet round lower edge. Embroider flowers in lazy daisy stitch round bottom. Trim with fringe through the last row of double crochet, using main and contrast wool together.

Japanese doll

She is wearing her kimono in the colour picture on page 99 but she took it off for us to take the picture on page 101

Materials: Two 2 oz. balls of Twilley's Stalite in Blue and I ball each in Gold, Black and green;
a pair of No. 12(1) knitting needles;
kapok for stuffing;
felt or wool for features, and flowers.

Tension: 7½ sts. and 10 rows to 1 inch.

Measurements: Height: 16 ins.

Abbreviations: See Page 10

DOLL

Skirt: Make two pieces. With Blue, cast on 37 sts. and knit 4 rows. **Next row:** Knit.
Next row: K.3, p.31, k.3. Rep. last 2 rows until work measures 8½ ins. from beg., ending with wrong side row.
Next row: K.1, (k.2 tog., k.1) 12 times.
Next row: Purl. Leave these two pieces on spare needle. (Each 25 sts.)
Main Part: * With Black cast on 13 sts. for base of left shoe. Work 8 rows st.st., increasing 1 st. at each end of first 2 rows and decreasing 1 st. at each end of last 2 rows. Cast off.
With Black, cast on 34 sts. for left shoe. Work 10 rows st.st. Beginning with a k. row, change to Gold and work 2 rows st.st. **Next row:** K.14, k.2 tog., k.2, k.2 tog., k.14. **Next row:** P.
Next row: K.13, k.2 tog., k.2, k.2 tog., k.13. **Next row:** Purl.
Next row: K.12, k.2 tog., k.2, k.2 tog., k.12. **Next row:** Purl.
Next row: K.2 tog., k.9, k.2 tog., k.2, k.2 tog., k.9, k.2 tog. (24 sts.) Cont. without further shaping until work measures 8 ins. from cast-on edge, ending

with a p. row. * Leave these sts. on a spare needle and rep. from * to * for right shoe, foot and leg. Change to Blue.
Next row: K.12, and leave these 12 sts. on a spare needle, k.12, cast on 1 then knit first 12 sts. from left leg, turn and leave rem. 12 sts. on a spare needle. Work on 25 sts. for Back of body. ** Work 1¾ ins. st.st., ending with a p. row. **Next row:** Place 25 sts. of one piece of skirt in front of sts. on needle, then knit both lots of sts. together, taking 1 st. from each needle together across the row. Work 1¼ ins. in st.st. beg. with a p. row. Cont. in st.st. and cast off 2 sts. at beg. of next 2 rows then dec. 1 st. at each end of every 3rd row until 9 sts. rem., ending with a k. row. Knit 3 rows.
Change to gold for head. **Next row:** k. twice into every st. to end of row. Cont. in st.st. and inc. 1 st. at each end of every alt. row until there are 28 sts. on needle. Cont. without further shaping until head measures 2½ ins. from beg. Now dec. 1 st. at each end of next and every alt. row until 16 sts. rem. Cast off. Return to rem. sts. and with right side facing, and Blue, knit 12 sts. from left leg, cast on 1, k.12 sts. from right leg and complete front as for back from **.
Arms:
With Gold, cast on 7 sts. and work 2 rows st.st., beg. with a k. row.
Next row: K.1, (inc. into next st.) 6 times. Work 3 rows st.st., beg. with a p. row. **Next row:** K.1, (inc. into next st., k.1) 6 times. (19 sts.) Cont. in st.st., beg. with a p. row until arm measures 4¾ ins. from cast on edge, ending with a k. row.
Next row: P.3, (inc. into next st., p.2) 5 times, p.1. Change to Blue and knit 4 rows. Now work in st.st., beg. with a k. row. Cast off 2 sts., at beg. of next 2 rows and then dec. 1 st. at each end of every alt. row until 4 sts. rem. Knit 1 row. Next row: (k.2 tog.) twice. Knit 1 row and cast off.

TO MAKE UP

Join leg seams. Sew bases into shoes. Join shaped top edges of arms to back and front, then join side and arm seams. Join head seams, leaving an opening at top to allow stuffing. Stuff firmly and join opening. Join the side seams of skirt, leaving 4 ins. open at lower edge for slits. With a quarter of remaining black yarn, wind an even hank 6 ins. in circumference using a small book or box which measures 6 ins. round. Slip hank off and wind a length of Black round the centre of hank to make the top knot. Wind the remaining Black into a hank 16 ins. in circumference. Slip off and place the yarn around the head. Arrange evenly over centre of head and sew neatly working from front to back. Twist the remainder into a bun and secure to back of head. Add top knot to top of head. Make flowers from scraps of felt and sew to hair. Cut features from scraps of felt and add to face, or embroider with scraps of yarn.

KIMONO

Main Part:

With Blue, cast on 133 sts. ** Knit 3 rows. Join in Green.

Next row: K.3 Blue, knit with Green to last 3 sts., join second ball of Blue, k.3 Blue. **Next row:** K.3 Blue, p. with Green to last 3 sts., k.3 Blue. Work 2 more rows in st.st. in Green, keeping 3 sts. at each end in Blue g.st. ** Now work in pattern.

1st row: (wrong side) With Blue, K.6, * insert needle through next st., 4 rows below (in first Green row) and knit through the st., drawing up a long loop, knit the next st. on needle still, then take the loop over this st., k.3, rep. from * to last 3 sts., k.3.

2nd row: With Blue, K.3, p. to last 3 sts., k.3. **3rd row:** With Blue, Knit.

4th row: As 2nd. **5th row:** K.3 Blue, k.1 Green, * with Green, insert needle through next st., 4 rows below (first Blue row) and knit through it, drawing up a long loop, knit next st. Still on needle then take loop over this st., k.3 Green, rep. from * to last 5 sts., with Green, insert needle through next st. 4 rows below as before, k.1 Green, 3 Blue. **6th row:** K.3 Blue, purl with Green to last 3 sts., k.3 Blue.

7th row: K.3 Blue, k. with Green to last 3 sts., k.3 Blue. **8th row:** As 6th. These 8 rows form the pattern.

Cont. in pattern until work measures $4\frac{3}{4}$ ins. from beg. ending with a 2nd or 6th patt. row.

Next row: With Blue, K.6, (k.1, k.2 tog.) to last 7 sts., k.7. Now rep. from ** to ** again, then work first 5 rows of pattern.

Divide for Armhole: K.3 Blue, with Green, p.19, cast off 7, p.35, cast off 7, p. 19, k.3 Blue. Work on last set of sts. for left front.

Keeping 3 sts. at front edge in Blue g.st., Work 1 row. **Next row:** Patt. to last 5 sts., p.2 tog., k.3 Blue. Now dec. in this way on every alt. row inside front border until 10 sts. remain. Cont. without further shaping in patt. with front border as before until work measures $9\frac{1}{2}$ ins. from cast on edge, ending at armhole.

Cast off 7 sts. at beg. of next row. Work $1\frac{1}{2}$ ins. g.st. in Blue on rem. 3 sts.

Rejoin yarn to centre 35 sts. for Back. Cont. in pattern excluding Blue g.st. borders until work measures $9\frac{1}{2}$ ins. from cast-on edge. Cast off 7 sts. at beg. of next 2 rows. Cast off rem. sts.

Rejoin yarn to rem. 22 sts. for right front. Keeping 3 sts. at front edge in Blue g.st., as before, work 1 row pattern. **Next row:** K.3 Blue, p.2 tog., patt. to end. Dec. in this way inside front border on every alt. row and complete to match left front.

Sleeves:

With Blue, cast on 51 sts. and knit 3 rows. Join in Green and work 4 rows st.st., beg. with a k. row. Now work in pattern.

1st row: (wrong side) With Blue, k.3,

* insert needle into next st. 4 rows below
as on main part, k.3, rep. from * to end.
Work 3 rows st.st. in Blue, beg. with a p.
row.

5th row: With Green, K.1, * insert needle
into next st. 4 rows below as before, k.3,
rep. from * to end, ending k.1. Work 3
rows st.st. in Green beg., with a p. row.
These 8 rows form the pattern. Cont.
until work measures $3\frac{1}{2}$ ins. from
cast-on edge.

To Shape Top: Cont. in patt. and cast off
4 sts. at beg. of next 10 rows. Cast off rem.
sts.

Waistband and Bow:
With Blue, cast on 32 sts. for waistband.
Work 8 ins. in st.st. Cast off. cast on 18
sts. for bow. **1st row:** K.

2nd row: K.4, p.10, k.4. Rep. last 2 rows
for 10 ins. Cast off.

TO MAKE UP

Join sleeve and shoulder seams. Set in
sleeves. Fold waistband in half and join
sides. Turn to right side and join ends.
Fold bow with ends at centre back and
stitch lightly. Gather centre of bow and
sew to one end of waistband. Sew three
press fasteners to ends of waistband and
fasten at centre back of kimono. Press
seams and edges.

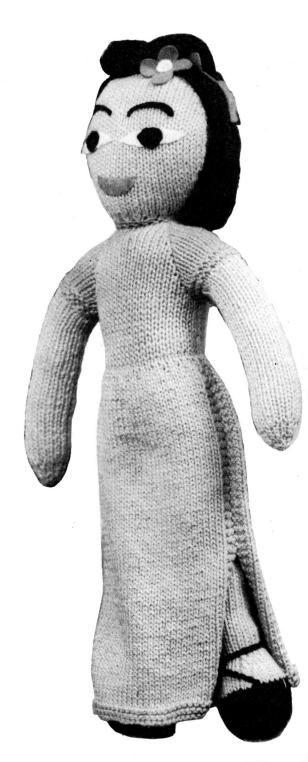

Charlie crocodile

He's too friendly to have crawled out of a swamp and will make a new friend for all the other jungle toys

Materials: 2 ozs. Twilley's Bubbly in green and yellow and 1 oz. orange; a pair of No. 10(3) knitting needles; scraps of felt for features; stuffing.

Tension: 5 sts., and 8 rows to 1 inch.

Measurements: Length: 14 ins.

Abbreviations: See Page 10

TO MAKE
Back:
Using yarn double and with green, cast on 8 sts. Working in st.st., inc. 1 st., at each end of every alt. row until there are 26 sts. on needle. Cont. without further shaping until piece measures 9 ins. from beg. Now dec. 1 st. at each end of next and every foll. 4th row until 2 sts. remain. Fasten off.
Front: As for Back using yellow double, but inc. only to 20 sts. then work without further shaping to 8½ ins. Dec. 1 st. at each end of next and every foll. 6th row until 2 sts. remain. Fasten off.
Mouth: Using orange double, cast on 6 sts. Work in st.st. and inc. 1 st. at each end of every alt. row until there are 22 sts. on needle. Cont. without further shaping until piece measures 4 ins. from beg., ending with a p. row. **Next row:** K.2, (k.2 tog., k.3) 4 times. Cont. without further shaping until piece measures 6½ ins. Now dec. 1 st. at each end of next and every alt. row until 6 sts. remain. Cast off.

Legs: Using 2 strands of green, cast on 6 sts. and work in st.st., Inc. 1 st. at each end of 2nd and 3rd rows. Cont. without further shaping until piece measures 2 ins. ending with a p. row. **Next row:** Cast on 6 sts., knit to end. Work 9 rows st.st., beg. with a p. row. Now dec. 1 st. at each end of next and beg. of foll. row. Cast off. Make another piece to match in green and two in yellow. Then work 2 in green and 2 in yellow but ending with a k. row before casting on 6 sts. Cont. to work to match in reverse.

TO MAKE UP
Join leg pieces matching pairs of green and yellow, leaving top of leg open. Stuff. Sew mouth to cast on ends of back and front. The wider end of mouth to back for 4 ins, then the narrower end to front for 4 ins. Join remaining edges of back and front, leaving 5 inches open at each side. Stuff body. Insert legs and join remaining side seams. Cut 4 lengths of white felt to make teeth and add to mouth. Cut two circles of black and white for eyes. Sew eyes to head.

Hula doll

With Jungle toys about there must be a lady in a grass skirt somewhere. She could have flowers in her hair and bead bangles and necklace, but not for a child still at the stage of swallowing small objects

Materials: One 50 gramme ball of Patons Double Knitting Wool in Brown; 1 ball of Limelight Double Crepe in Nectarine; 1 ball in Capstan in Gold and Emerald; 1 ball Doublet in Black; a pair of No. 9(4) knitting needles; a No. 4.50 mm crochet hook; kapok for stuffing.

Tension: $5\frac{1}{2}$ sts. and $7\frac{1}{2}$ rows to 1 inch in Double knitting.

Measurements: Height: 15 ins.

Abbreviations: See Page 10

BODY AND LEGS

Cast on 7 sts. in Brown and work in st.st. for 40 rows. Break yarn. Make another piece to match. Knit across first 7 sts., cast on 3 sts., and work across second set of 7 sts. Work 35 rows on these 17 sts. Cast off. Make another piece in the same way. Join the two pieces together, leaving neck open. Stuff firmly and sew up neck opening.

ARMS

Cast on 12 sts. in brown and work 32 rows in st.st. Cast off. Make another piece to match. Join the long edges of each piece, stuff firmly and sew to body.

HANDS

Cast on 14 sts. in Brown and work 14 rows in st.st. Cast off. Make another piece to match. Join seams and stuff firmly and

sew to arms.

HEAD

Make two pieces, one in Brown and one in Black for back of head.
Cast on 8 sts. and work in st.st. Inc. 1 st. at each end of 3rd and foll. alt. rows until there are 28 sts. Work 15 rows straight.
Next row: K.2 tog. along row. Work 1 row
Next row: K.2 tog. along row. Cast off.
Join the two pieces together leaving cast on edges open for neck. Stuff firmly and sew to body.

FEET

Cast on 26 sts. in Brown and work 8 rows in st.st. Cast off. Join bottom and side seams. Place legs inside this casing at the back. Stuff and sew up the front seams. Sew the top of the sides and back to legs.

GRASS SKIRT

With Green wool, crochet a 6 inch chain. Work in slip stitch along the chain. Fasten around waist. Make 22 chains in Green and 22 in gold in double crochet each 5 ins. long. Take one strand in each colour in turn and attach to waistband, working all round waist.

NECK GARLAND

Cast on 46 sts. in Nectarine and make a loop row thus:
Insert needle into first st. Wind yarn over point of needle and first two fingers of left hand 3 times, then over needle again. Draw the loop through the st. and place loops back on left hand needle. Knit the 3 loops together through back of loops. Cont. in this way to end of row. Cast off.
For ankles and wrists, make a garland for each by casting on 12 sts. in Nectarine and working a row of loop st. as for neck garland.

Fasten garlands round neck, ankles and wrists.

For the Flower make by casting on 30 sts. in Nectarine and working 1 loop row but winding the yarn round 3 fingers instead of two. Cast off. Gather into a flower shape and sew to side front of head.

HAIR

Cut Black yarn into 40 lengths each 18 ins. long. Divide into groups of 10. Fold in half and join 3 groups to the back of head at seam and one group over the top at centre front on the seam. Embroider features in Black and Nectarine.

Home comforts

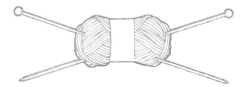

A collection of exciting items to make, most of them just a
straight piece of knitting. It is what you do with the piece that
matters, and the colours you choose to enhance your home.
The Aran cushions and lampshades are very effective and an
unusual use for these traditional stitches. Tea, coffee and egg
cosies are always useful and a hand knitted bedspread will last
a lifetime. The cheerful cushions will do good service in garden
or playroom, or for sheer comfort by the fire. The simple bath
mat, so quick to make, would also be as good as a bedside rug

Coffee pot cosy

Almost a straight piece and the stitch makes the pointed edge. As long as you have enough wool to work two rows, you could use as many odd pieces of wool as you like

Materials 2 ozs. Lee Target Motoravia D.K. in Brown and 1 oz. each of yellow, emerald and cream; a pair of No. 9(4) knitting needles.

Tension: 6 sts. and 8 rows to 1 inch.

Measurements: All round: 16 ins.; Height: 10 ins.

Abbreviations: See page 10

TO MAKE

Cast on 51 sts. with Brown and knit 1 row. Now begin pattern.

1st row: (Right side) with yellow. K.1, sl.1, k.1, p.s.s.o., * k.9, sl.2, k.1, p.2 s.s.o., rep. from * to last 12 sts., k.9, k.2 tog., k.1

2nd row: K.1, * p.1, k.4, (k.1, w.o.n., k.1) all into next st., k.4, rep. from * to last 2 sts., p.1, k.1.

3rd and 4th rows: With Brown as 1st and 2nd. **5th and 6th rows:** With Emerald as 1st and 2nd.

7th and 8th: As 3rd and 4th.

9th and 10th rows: With cream as 1st and 2nd. Continue in this way, working 2 rows in Brown and 2 rows in each of the other colours in turn, until piece measures 7½ ins. Change to Brown and work 4 more rows in pattern. **Next row:** K.1, p.1, * k.9, p.1, rep. from * to end.

Next row: K.1, k.2 tog., * k.7, sl.1, k.2 tog., p.s.s.o., rep. from * to last 10 sts., k.7, k.2 tog., k.1.

Next row: K.1, p.1, * k.7, p.1, rep. from * to end.

Next row: K.1, k.2 tog., * k.5, sl.1, k.2 tog., p.s.s.o., rep. from * to last 8 sts., k.5, k.2 tog., k.1.

Next row: K.1, p.1, * k.5, p.1, rep. from * to last st., k.1. Now work 17 rows K.3, p.3 rib. Change to a contrast colour and work 1 row and then cast off. Make another piece to match.

TO MAKE UP

Press pieces. Join side seams, leaving gaps for spout and handle. Press seams. Turn ribbed top down to right side.

Bath mat

Big needles and thick yarn make a quick job of this mat. It's easy too, so any beginner can manage it

Materials: 5 hanks of Twilley's 747 Orlon Sayelle; a pair of ½ inch Whizz pins; a crochet hook No. 4.50.

Tension: 3 sts. to 2 ins.

Measurements: 31 by 20 ins., excluding fringe.

Abbreviations: See Page 10

TO MAKE

Cast on 30 sts. loosely. K.2 rows.
3rd row: Sl.1, * K.1, k.1b. rep. from * to last st., k.1.
4th row: Sl.1, * k. the slip thread of previous row with the st. above it, k.1, rep. from * to last st., k.1.
5th row: Sl.1, * k.1 b., k.1, rep. from * to last st., k.1.
6th row: Sl.1, * K.1, k. the slip thread of the previous row with the st. above it, rep. from * to last st., k.1. Cont. in patt. from 3rd row until work measures 30 ins. from beg. Then slipping the first st. on each row. K. 2 rows. Cast off loosely. Fringe the narrow ends.

Oblong cushion and tall lampshade

Really smart to bring a touch of real craftsmanship to the things you can make for your home. Cream Aran wool was used and is most effective. In the lampshade, when the light is on, the result is even better

Materials: Six 2 oz. balls of Lister Aran Knitting Wool for cushion and 4 balls for lampshade;
a pair each of Nos. 7(6) and 9(4) knitting needles;
a cable needle;
a lampshade frame 19 ins. in circumferance and 13½ ins. deep;
cushion pad to fit;
a No. 4.00 m.m. crochet hook.

Tension: 5 sts. and 7 rows to 1 inch.

Measurements: Cushion: 12 by 18 ins. Lampshade as size of frame given.

Abbreviations: See Page 10

CUSHION
With No. 9(4) needles, cast on 90 sts. and knit 1 row.
Next row: K.3, *(p.f.b., p.2) 3 times, (k.1, p.1, 3-in-1, p.1, k.1, p.1) twice, k.1, p.1, 3-in-1, k.1, rep. from * twice more, (p.f.b., p.2) 3 times, k.3. (120 sts.) Change to No. 7(6) needles and patt.
1st row: K.2, p.1, * k.12, p.22, rep. from * twice more, k.12, p.1, k.2.
2nd row: K.3, * p.12, k.1, (3-in-1, p.3 tog.) 5 times, k.1, rep. from * twice more, p.12, k.3.
3rd row: As 1st. **4th row:** K.3, * p.12, k.1, (p.3 tog., 3-in-1) 5 times, k.1, rep. from * twice more, p.12, k.3.
5th row: K.2, p.1, * C6B., C6F., p.22, rep. from * twice more, C6B., C6F., p.1, k.2. **6th row:** As 2nd.
7th row: As 1st. **8th row:** As 4th

9th row: As 1st. **10th row:** As 2nd.
11th row: As 5th. **12th row:** As 4th.
13th to 20th row: Rep. from 1st to 4th rows inclusive twice. **21st row:** K.2, p.1, * C6F., C6B., p.22, rep. from * twice more, C6F., C6B., p.1, k.2.
22nd row: As 2nd. **23rd row:** As 1st.
24th row: As 4th. **25th row:** As 1st.
26th row: As 2nd. **27th row:** As 21st.
28th row: As 4th. These 28 rows form one pattern. Cont. until 6th patt. is completed, then work first 3 rows again. Change to No. 9(4) needles.
Next row: K.3, *(p.2 tog., p.2) 3 times, (k.1, p.3 tog., k.1, p.1, k.1, p.1) twice, k.1, p.3 tog., k.2., rep. from * twice more, (p.2 tog., p.2) 3 times, k.3. Cast off tightly.

TO MAKE UP
Fold work in half and join three sides. Insert cushion pad. Work 1 row double crochet through two thicknesses along one end, turn with 1 chain. Now make fringe thus: With a piece of cardboard 1¾ ins. wide, hold card above work, insert hook into first double crochet, wind wool round card and then over hook and draw loop through, complete the double crochet. Cont. to end of row, slipping some loops off card as work progresses. Work other side to match.

LAMPSHADE
With No. 9(4) needles, cast on 95 sts. and work 2 rows g.st.
Next row: K.1, *(k.1, p.1, 3-in-1, p.1, k.1, p.1) twice, k.2, (p.f.b., p.2) 3 times, rep. from * to last 2 sts., k.2. (123 sts.) Change to No. 7(6) needles and patt.
1st row: K.1, p.1, * k.12, p.18, rep. from * to last st., k.1.
2nd row: K.1, * k.1, (3-in-1, p.3 tog.) 4 times, k.1, p.12, rep. from * to last 2 sts., k.2. **3rd row:** As 1st.
4th row: K.1, * k.1, (p.3 tog., 3-in-1) 4

times, k.1, p.12, rep. from * to last 2 sts., k.2. **5th row:** K.1, p.1, * C6B., C6F., p.18, rep. from * to last st., k.1. Cont. in this way, working in these positions as on the cushion until 3 patterns have been completed. Repeat first 3 rows again. Change to No. 9(4) needles.

Next row: K.1, * (k.1, p.3 tog., k.1, p.1, k.1, p.1) twice, k.2, (p.2 tog., p.2) 3 times, rep. from * to last 2 sts., k.2. Work 2 rows in g.st. Cast off tightly.

TO MAKE UP

Join side edges. Fit over lampshade frame. Work 1 row double crochet all round top and bottom edges, taking in the edge of frame.

Bedspread and cushion in squares

Make use of all those odd ounces or plan to a careful colour scheme and buy the wool bit by bit. You will have a bedspread to last a lifetime and a cheerful cushion to stand up to hard use

Materials: The bedspread and cushion are made in Double knitting wool on No. 10(3) needles.

Tension: 6 sts. and 8 rows to 1 inch over stocking stitch.

Measurements: The squares are 5 inches square and approx. 3 squares can be made from 1 oz. of wool. The bedspread measures 90 inches by 60 ins. excluding the fringe. The fringe used approx. 7 ozs. of wool in odd balls.
Note: To obtain these measurements any stitch may be used and it is essential to obtain the correct tension for the stitches given in this pattern. It is wise to work a tension square when undertaking any knitting. Collect 5 inch tension squares every time you use the same thickness of wool, until enough have been collected. In this way, both variety in stitch and colour will be achieved. In the centre of the bedspread there is a panel of 24 two and three colour squares. These use up the oddments of wool one collects. They are all in star stitch, which was also used for a cushion, and a bag.

STITCHES USED
Star Stitch
With No. 10(3) needles and first colour, cast on 33 sts.
1st row: (wrong side) Purl.
2nd row: K.2, * w.r.n., k.3, pass first of the 3 knit sts. over 2nd and 3rd sts., rep. from * to last st., k.1. **3rd row:** With second colour, P.
4th row: K.1, * k.3, pass the first of 3 knit sts. over 2nd and 3rd sts., w.r.n., rep. from * to last 2 sts., k.2. Rep. rows 1 to 4 for 5 ins.
Any number of colours may be used, changing colour on odd rows.

Moss Knit Rib
Cast on 32 sts.
1st row: * K.3, p.1, rep. from * to end.
2nd row: * K.2, p.1, k.1, rep. from * to end. Rep. these 2 rows for 5 ins.

Crossed Rib
Cast on 33 sts.
1st row: *(P.1, k.1) twice, rep. from * to last st., p.1.
2nd row: *(K.1, p.1) twice, rep. from * to last st., k.1. **3rd row:** As 1st.
4th row: As 2nd.
5th row: * P.1, cross 2R by knitting the 3rd st., p. 2nd st., and k. first st., then let all 3 drop from left hand needle. Rep. from * to last st., p.1.
6th row: As 2nd. Rep. these 6 rows for 5 ins.

Laburnham Stitch

Cast on 32 sts.

1st row: P.2, * w.fwd., sl.1 purlwise, w.b., k.2 tog., p.s.s.o., w.r.n., p.2, rep. from * to end.

2nd row: * K.2, p. into front and back of next st., p.1, rep. from * to last 2 sts., k.2.

3rd row: P.2, * k.3, p.2, rep. from * to end.

4th row: * K.2, p.3, rep. from * to last 2 sts., k.2.

Rep. these 4 rows for 5 ins.

Campanular Stitch

Cast on 32 sts.,

1st row: K.1, * k.3, p.2, rep. from * to last st., k.1.

2nd row: K.1, * k.2, p.3, rep. from * to last st., k.1.

3rd row: As 1st. **4th row:** As 2nd

5th row: K.1, * w.r.n., sl.1, k.2 tog., p.s.s.o., w.r.n., p.2, rep. from * to last st., k.1. **6th row:** As 2nd. Rep. these 6 rows for 5 ins.

Alternating Link Stitch

1st row: Cast on 32 sts. * P.5, k.1, p.1, rep. from * to last 4 sts., p.4.

2nd and 4th rows: K.4, * k.1, p.1, k.5, rep. from * to end.

3rd row: * P.5, k.1, p.1, rep. from * to last 4 sts., p.4.

5th and 7th rows: * P.4, k.1, p.1, k.1, rep. from * to last 4 sts., p.4.

6th row: * K.4, p.1, k.1, p.1, rep. from * to last 4 sts., k.4.

8th row: As 2nd.

Rep. these 8 rows for 5 ins.

TO MAKE UP BEDSPREAD

Pin out squares and press. Join in strips of 12 squares. Join strips together matching corners carefully. Press seams. Add fringing.

CUSHION

Join squares together in strips of 3. Join three strips together for each side of cushion. Press pieces. Cut lining to match and make up cushion pad. Join three sides of knitted pieces and insert cushion pad. Close fourth side. Make a thick twisted cord using two colours and sew round edge of cushion.

This will make a cushion 15 inches square.

Hexagon patchwork bedspread and cushion

The beauty of patchwork is that you can make the pieces when and where you like. They arc small to carry and can be put together when you have time. See page 13 for how to do Swiss darning.

Materials: Both bedspread and cushion are made in Twilley's Afghan wool in five colours.
No. 10(3) knitting needles.
Lining and stuffing for cushion.

Tension: 6 sts. and 8 rows to 1 inch.

Measuresments: Each six sided patch is 6 inches wide and 6 ins. long. The finished bedspread measures 75 ins. long and 62 ins. wide.

Abbreviations: See Page 10

Note: This design requires 48 yellow patches, and 48 in rust, 30 brown, 24 white, 16 green in garter stitch. 12 white patches in stocking stitch and 2 in brown for the embroidered patches and 2 half patches in each colour in garter stitch. Assorted colours could be used and the patches arranged in any design to please the owner. 1 oz. makes 4 patches.

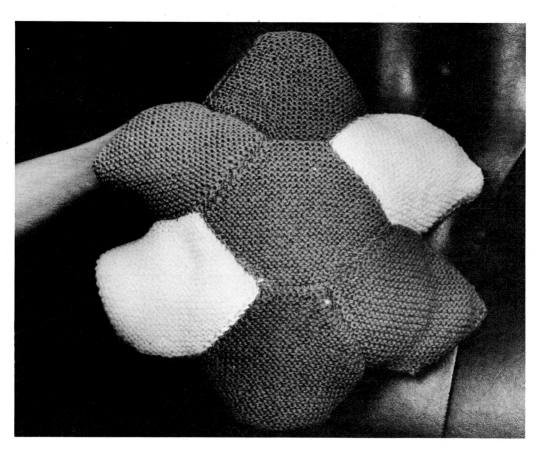

TO MAKE

Garter Stitch Patch

Cast on 12 sts. and k. 1 row.

2nd row: K.1, p.u.k., k.10, p.u.k., k.1.

3rd and all alt. rows: K.

4th row: K.1, p.u.k., k.12, p.u.k., k.1.

6th row: K.1, p.u.k., k.14, p.u.k., k.1.

Cont. to inc. in this way until there are 36 sts. on needle. Knit 1 row then dec. 1 st. at each end of every alt. row until 12 sts. remain. Cast off.

Stocking stitch Patch

Cast on 12 sts. and k. 1 row.

2nd row: As for garter st. patch.

3rd and alt. rows: K.2, p. to last 2 sts., k.2.

Continue to inc. to 36 sts. and dec. back to 12 sts. as for garter stitch patch. Cast off.

Half Patches

Cast on 36 sts. and work decrease half of garter stitch patch.

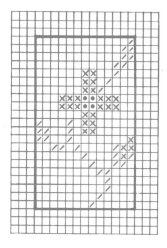

✕ Rust or Yellow
╱ Green
• Brown or Rust

TO MAKE UP

Press pieces. Whatever design is followed, the end result is neatest if the patches are joined first in strips and then the strips joined together.

Make 4 strips of 12 patches in yellow; 4 strips of 12 patches in rust; 2 strips of 12 patches in brown and 2 strips the same in white, garter stitch.

Embroider white stocking stitch patches and two brown with flower motif, follow Chart using oddments of wool. For centre panel make one strip of 12 patches thus: * 2 green, 1 white embroidered, 1 green, 1 white embroidered, rep. from * 2 green. Make another strip to match. The centre strip is made thus: 2 brown garter st., 1 white embroidered, 1 brown garter st., 1 white embroidered, 1 brown embroidered, 1 brown garter st., 1 embroidered brown, 1 white embroidered, 1 brown garter st., 1 white embroidered, 1 brown garter st.

Join strips in this order, starting with yellow, rust, yellow, brown, white, rust, green and white embroidered, the centre strip of brown and white. Then continue to match other side. Add small tassels to points along the sides and add half patches where required at top and bottom. Press. Take 14 patches for cushion. Make one strip of three patches, joining cast on edges to cast off edges. Join two patches by cast on edges and fit in to one side of strip of three. Make other side to match. Make another piece in the same way.

Cut lining material from paper pattern made from completed knitted piece. Make two pieces and join carefully, leaving small part open for stuffing. Stuff, taking care to keep shape of points. Close opening. Make up knitted pieces, leaving opening to insert pad. Insert pad and close opening.

Striped cushion

Straight knitting again and three toning colours, but again, the choice is yours.

Materials: 5 ozs. Lee Target Motoravia Double Knitting Wool in Brown and 2 ozs. each in cream and gold;
a pair of No. 7(6) knitting needles;
lining and stuffing.

Tension: 5¼ sts. and 7 rows to 1 inch.

Measurements: Approx. 15 ins. wide by 22 ins. long.

Abbreviations: See Page 10

TO MAKE
With Brown, cast on 72 sts. and work in st.st. throughout. Work in stripes. * 14 rows Brown, 1 inch each in cream, gold and cream. * Rep. from * to * then repeat 14 rows Brown. Cast off. Make another piece to match. Cut lining to match.
Join 3 sides and stuff. Close 4th side. Make up knitted pieces to match, taking care to match stripes. Insert the cushion and close 4th side. Fringe short ends with remaining wool, using 4 strands each 4 ins. long for each tassel.

Square cushion and large lampshade

Just a different shape for both and different stitches too. If you make them as gifts, you will find it hard to part with them

Materials: Eight 2 oz. balls of Lister Aran knitting wool for cushion cover and 6 balls for the lampshade;
a pair each of Nos. 7(6) and 9(4) knitting needles;
a cable needle;
a No. 4.00 m.m crochet hook;
a lampshade frame 9 ins. deep by 44 ins. circumference;
2½ yds. wool braid to match;
½ yd. press stud tape.

Tension: 5 sts. and 7 rows to 1 inch over st.st. on No. 7(6) needles.

Measurements: Cushion cover: 17 ins. square.;
Lampshade as size of frame.

Abbreviations: See Page 10

CUSHION COVER

With No. 9(4) needles, cast on 101 sts. and knit 1 row.
Next row: K.3, * p.1, (p.f.b., p.1) twice, k.f.b., (p.2, p.f.b.) 7 times, p.4, k.f.b., (p.1, p.f.b.) twice, p.1, * k.8, p.2, k.1, p.2, k.8, rep. from * to *, k.3. (127 sts.)
Change to No. 7(6) needles and patt.
1st row: K.2, p.1, * k.7, p.2, k.32, p.2, k.7, * p.8, cross 5, p.8, rep. from * to *, p.1, k.2.
2nd row: K.3, * p.7, k.2, p.32, k.2, p.7, *, k.8, p.2, k.1, p.2, k.8, rep. from * to *, k.3. **3rd row:** K.2, p.1, *CP7, p.2, (C4B, C4F) 4 times, p.2, CP7, * p.7, C3R, p.1, C3L, p.7, rep. from * to *, p.1, k.2.
4th row: K.3, * p.7, k.2, p.32, k.2, p.7, * k.7, p.2, k.3, p.2, k.7, rep. from * to *, k.3. **5th row:** K.2, p.1, * k.7, p.2, k.32, p.2, k.7, * p.6, C3R, p.3, C3L, p.6, rep. from * to * p.1, k.2.
6th row: K.3, * p.7, k.2, p.32, k.2, p.7, * k.6, p.2, k.5, p.2, k.6, rep. from * to * k.3. **7th row:** K.2, p.1, * CP7, p.2, (C4F, C4B) 4 times, p.2, CP7 *, p.5, C3R, p.2, MB, p.2, C3L, p.5, rep. from * to *, p.1, k.2.
8th row: K.3, * p.7, k.2, p.32, k.2, p.7, * k.5, p.2, k.7, p.2, k.5.; rep. from * to *, k.3. These 8 rows complete the patt. for double honeycomb and claw patt. panels. Cont. to keep these correct and at the same time, cont. with diamond panel in the centre.
9th row: K.2, p.1, patt. 50, p.4, C3R, p.7, C3L, p.4, patt. 50, p.1, k.2.
10th row: K.3, patt. 50, k.4, p.2, k.9, p.2, k.4, patt. 50, k.3.
11th row: K.2, p.1, patt. 50, p.3, C3R, p.2, MB, p.3, MB, p.2, C3L, p.3, patt. 50, p.1, k.2.
12th row: K.3, patt. 50, k.3, p.2, k.11, p.2, k.3, patt. 50, k.3.
13th row: K.2, p.1, patt. 50, p.2, C3R, p.11, C3L, p.2, patt. 50, p.1, k.2.
14th row: K.3, patt. 50, k.2, p.2, k.13, p.2, k.2, patt. 50, k.3. **15th row:** K.2, p.1,

120

patt. 50, p.2, k.2, p.2, MB, p.7, MB, p.2, k.2, p.2, patt. 50, p.1, k.2.

16th row: As 14th. **17th row:** K.2, p.1, patt. 50, p.2, C3L, p.11, C3R, p.2, patt. 50, p.1, k.2. **18th row:** As 12th.

19th row: K.2, p.1, patt. 50, p.3, C3L, p.2, MB, p.3, MB, p.2, C3R, p.3, patt. 50, p.1, k.2. **20th row:** As 10th.

21st row: K.2, p.1, patt. 50, p.4, C3L, p.7, C3R, p.4, patt. 50, p.1, k.2.

22nd row: As 8th. **23rd row:** K.2, p.1, patt. 50, p.5, C3L, p.2, MB, p.2, C3R, p.5, patt. 50, p.1, k.2.

24th row: As 6th. **25th row:** K.2, p.1, patt. 50, p.6, C3L, p.3, C3R, p.6, patt. 50, p.1, k.2. **26th row:** As 4th

27th row: K.2, p.1, patt. 50, p.7, C3L, p.1, C3R, p.7, patt. 50, p.1, k.2.

28th row: As 2nd. These 28 rows form patt. for diamond panel. Cont. until 8 complete patts. have been worked in this panel. Work 1st and 2nd rows again. Change to No. 9(4) needles.

Next row: K.2, p.1, * k.1, (k.2 tog., k.1) twice, p.2 tog., (k.2, k.2 tog.) 7 times, k.4, p.2 tog., (k.1, k.2 tog.) twice, k.1, * p.8, k.2, p.1, k.2, p.8, rep. from * to * p.1, k.2. Cast off.

TO MAKE UP

Fold work in half with wrong side out and join cast on and cast off edge, Press seam. Turn right side out. Along one side edge, work a row of double crochet through both thicknesses. Work a row of double crochet round the 2 sides of other edge. Sew press stud tape to opening. Insert cushion and fasten.

LAMPSHADE

With No. 9(4) needles, cast on 131 sts. and work 3 rows g.st.

Next row: K.1, * k.8, p.2, k.1, p.2, k.8, (p.1, p.f.b.) twice, p.1, k.f.b., (p.2, p.f.b., 9 times, p.4, k.f.b., (p.1, p.f.b.) twice, p.1, rep. from * once, k.2. (161 sts.) Change to No. 7(6) needles and patt.

1st row: K.1, p.1, * k.7, p.2, k.40, p.2, k.7, p.8, cross 5, p.8, rep. from * once, k.1.

2nd row: K.1, * k.8, p.2, k.1, p.2, k.8, p.7, k.2, p.40, k.2, p.7, rep. from * once, k.2. **3rd row:** K.1, p.1, * CP7, p.2, (C4B, C4F) 5 times, p.2, CP7, p.7, C3R, p.1, C3L, p.7, rep. from * once, k.1. Cont. in patt. as now set working 40 sts. in double honeycomb and other panels as on cushion, until 58 rows have been worked in patt. Change to No. 9(4) needles.

Next row: K.1, p.1, * k.1, (k.2 tog., k.1) twice, p.2 tog., (k.2, k.2 tog.) 9 times, k.4, p.2 tog., (k.1, k.2 tog.) twice, k.1, p.8, k.2, p.1, k.2, p.8, rep. from * once, k.1. Change to g.st., and work 3 rows. Cast off. Make another piece to match.

TO MAKE UP

Place pieces together and join into a circle. Press seams. Fit over frame, placing seams over 2 of side supports. Catch the seams to supports. Fold g.st. edges over top and bottom of frame and catch down firmly, so that cover is stretched over frame slightly. Sew braid to top and bottom.

Fringed cushion in star stitch

Just two squares in a pretty stitch. Three colours were used for this one, but you could use as many colours as you like, changing every two rows

Materials 2 ozs. each of Lee Target Motoravia Double Knitting Wool in White, mauve and blue; a pair of No. 9(4) knitting needles, lining material; stuffing.

Tension: 6 sts. and 6 rows to 1 inch over pattern.

Measurements: 12 inch square.

Abbreviations: See page 10

With Mauve, cast on 72 sts. and work in Star stitch for 12½ ins.

1st row: (wrong side) Purl.
2nd row: K.2, * w.r.n., k.3, pass first of 3 knit sts. over 2nd and 3rd sts., rep. from * to last st., k.1. Change to White.
3rd row: Purl.
4th row: K.1, * k.3, pass first of 3 knit sts. over 2nd and 3rd sts., w.r.n., rep. from * to last 2 sts., k.2. Change to Blue and work 1st and 2nd rows again. Continue to work in patt. in this way, working 2 rows in each colour in turn. When work measures 12½ ins. Cast off. Make another piece to match.

TO MAKE UP
Cut two pieces of lining to match and join three seams. Stuff and close fourth side. Join knitted pieces in same way. Insert cushion into knitted cover and join fourth seam of cover. Fringe all round with remaining wool.

Tea, coffee and egg cosies

Matching set of cosies in traditional Aran stitches. Use them to keep things warm for breakfast or make them for a friend

Materials: 5 ozs. Lister Lavenda Double Knitting Wool for Tea or Coffee Cosy and 2 ozs. for a pair of Egg Cosies; a pair each of Nos. 9(4), and 11(2) knitting needles; a cable needle; a No. 3.50 m.m. crochet hook; 1 yd. single sided quilted fabric to line Tea and Coffee cosies; sewing silk.

Tension: 6½ sts. and 9 rows to 1 inch.

Measurements: Tea cosy: Width: 13 ins.; depth: 9 ins.; Coffee cosy: Width: 10 ins.; depth: 13 ins.; egg cosies: Depth: 5 ins.

Abbreviations: See Page 10

TEA COSY

Front: With No. 11(2) needles, cast on 87 sts. and work in rib.
1st row: K.2, * p.1, k.1, rep. from * to last st., k.1.
2nd row: K.1, * p.1, k.1, rep. from * to end. Rep. these 2 rows twice more, then 1st row again.
Next row: K.f.b., k.14, * p.1, (p.f.b., p.1) twice, k.f.b., (p.2, p.f.b.) 5 times, p.4, k.f.b., rep. from * once, p.1, (p.f.b., p.1) twice, k.14, k.f.b. Change to No. 9(4) needles. Now begin pattern.
1st row: (K.1 t.b.l., p.1) 8 times, * k.7, p.2, (TR., TL.) 4 times, p.2, rep. from * once, k.7, (p.1, k.1 t.b.l.) 8 times.
2nd row: K.16, * p.7, k.2, p.24, k.2, rep. from * once, p.7, k.16.
3rd row: (K.1 t.b.l., p.1) 8 times, * TR., k.1, TL., p.2, (TL., TR.) 4 times, p.2., rep. from * once, TR., k.1, TL., (p.1, k.1 t.b.l.) 8 times.
4th row: As 2nd. These 4 rows form one pattern. Cont. until work measures 5 ins. from beg. Now dec. 1 st. at each end of next row, then work 3 rows straight. Rep. last 4 rows 3 times more. Dec. 1 st. at each end of next row then work 1 row straight. Rep. last 2 rows 3 times more. Cast off 2 sts. at beg. of next 4 rows. Now cast off 3 sts. at beg. of next 4 rows and then cast off 6 sts. at beg. of next 4 rows. Now cast off tightly over the honeycomb panels.
Back: Work as for Front.

TO MAKE UP

Fold quilting in half with wadding inside and cut a section for Back in double thickness and one to match for Front. Join double sections together round side and top edges through four thicknesses. Join the knitted sections and insert lining. Turn ½ inch in all round lower edges and slip stitch to wrong side of first pattern row, leaving ribbing free.

COFFEE COSY

Front: With No. 11(2) needles, cast on 65 sts. and work 7 rows in rib as for Tea Cosy. **Next row:** K.f.b., k.16, rep. from * in same row as for tea cosy once, p.1, (p.f.b., p.1) twice, k.16, k.f.b. Change to No. 9(4) needles and pattern.
1st row: (K.1 t.b.l., p.1) 9 times, k.7, p.2, (TR., TL.) 4 times, p.2, k.7, (p.1, k.1, t.b.l.) 9 times
2nd row: K.18, p.7, k.2, p.24, k.2, p.7, k.18.
3rd row: (K.1 t.b.l., p.1) 9 times, TR., k.1, TL., p.2, (TL.,TR.) 4 times, p.2, TR., k.1, TL.; (p.1, k.1 t.b.l.) 9 times.
4th row: As 2nd. These 4 rows form the pattern. Cont. in pattern until work measures 10 ins. from beg. Dec. 1 st. at each end of next row, then work 3 rows straight. Rep. last 4 rows once. Dec. 1 st. at each end of next row, then work 1 row straight. Rep. last 2 rows twice more. Cast off 2 sts. at beg. of next 6 rows, then cast off 4 sts. at beg. of next 2 rows, then 6 sts. at beg. of next 2 rows. Cast off rem. sts. tightly over honeycomb panels.
Back: Work as for Front. Make up as for Tea Cosy.

EGG COSY

With No. 11(2) needles, cast on 55 sts. and work in rib as for tea cosy for 5 rows.
Next row: K.f.b., k.10, p.1, (p.f.b., p.1) twice, k.23, p.1, (p.f.b., p.1) twice, k.10, k.f.b., Change to No. 9(4) needles and pattern.
1st row: (K.1 t.b.l., p.1) 6 times, k.7, (p.1, k.1 t.b.l.) 11 times, p.1, k.7, (p.1, k.1 t.b.l.) 6 times.
2nd row: K.12, p.7, k.23, p.7, k.12. Cont. to keep panels of 12 sts. at each end of row and 23 sts. at centre in Rice stitch as on these 2 rows.
3rd row: RS.12, TR., k.1, TL., RS.23, TR., k.1, TL., RS.12.
4th row: As 2nd. Rep. these 4 rows 4 times more, then 1st, 2nd and 3rd rows again.
Next row: K.10, k.2 tog., p.7, k.2 tog. t.b.l., k.19, k.2 tog., p.7, k.2 tog. t.b.l., k.10.
Next row: RS.9, p.2 tog. t.b.l., k.7, p.2 tog., RS.17, p.2 tog. t.b.l., k.7, p.2 tog., RS.9.
Next row: K.8, k.2 tog., p.7, k.2 tog. t.b.l., k.15, k.2 tog., p.7, k.2 tog. t.b.l., k.8. Cont. to dec. in same positions on next 5 rows, keeping claw pattern correct.
Next row: K.1, (w.fwd., k.2 tog.) 14 times. Change to No. 11(2) needles and beg. with 1st row, work 4 rows in rib. Cast off in rib.
Join sides and press seam. With double wool, make a length of crochet chain about 14 ins. long. Thread through holes at top and draw up and tie in a bow.

Oblong aran cushion

If you want to master Aran knitting there's no better way than making a straight practice piece. What better use than a husky cushion, it makes the job worth while

Materials: 5 balls of Mahony's Blarney Bainin;
a pair each of Nos. 7(6) and 8(5) knitting needles;
a cushion to fit;
a cable needle

Tension: 9½ sts. to 2 inches on No. 7(6) needles.

Measurements: To fit 14 by 18 inch cushion.

Abbreviations: See page 10

TO MAKE
With No. 8(5) needles, cast on 94 sts. and p.1 row. Change to No. 7(6) needles and k.1 row, then cont. in patt.
1st row: P.5, * C2B., C2F., p.6, rep. from * ending last rep. p.5.
2nd row: K.5, * p.b.1, k.2, p.b.1, k.6, rep. from * ending last rep. k.5.
3rd row: P.4, * C2B, p.2, C2F., p.4, rep. from * to end.
4th and every wrong side row: K. all sts. purled in previous row and work p.b.1 into the k.b.1 sts.
5th row: P.3, * C2B., p.4, C2F., p.2, rep. from * to last st., p.1,
7th row: P.2, * C2B., p.6, C2F., rep. from * to last 2 sts., p.2.
9th row: P.2, * C2F., p.6, C2B., rep. from * to last 2 sts., p.2.
11th row: P.3, * C2F., p.4, C2B., p.2, rep. from * to last st., p.1.
13th row: P.4, * C2F., p.2, C2B., p.4, rep. from * to end.
15th row: P.5, * C2F., C2B., p.6, rep. from * ending last rep. p.5. **16th row:** As

4th. Change to No. 8(5) needles.
17th row: P. **18th and 19th rows:** K.
20th row: P. Change to No. 7(6) needles.
21st row: K. **22nd row:** P.6, (p. twice into next st., p.2) 27 times, p. twice into next st., p.6. **23rd row:** P.2, * C4B., C4F., p.2, rep. from * to end.
24th row: K.2, (p.8, k.2) 12 times.
25th row: P.2, (k.8, p.2) 12 times.
26th to 28th rows: Rep. 24th and 25th, then 24th row again.
29th row: P.2, * C4F., C4B., p.2 to end. Change to No.8(5) needles.
30th row: P.6, (p.2 tog., p.2) 27 times, p.2 tog., p.6.
31st row: K. **32nd and 33rd rows:** P. Change to No. 7(6) needles. **34th row:** K. Rep. these 34 rows once more then rows 1 to 16 again. Change to No. 8(5) needles and p. 1 row and then k. 1 row. Cast off. Make another piece to match.

TO MAKE UP
Press pieces on wrong side with a damp cloth and a hot iron. Join three sides then insert cushion. Join 4th side. Make a crochet chain cord, using 3 strands of wool together, long enough to fit round cushion. Sew to seam all round.